Cheese And Charcuterie Board Books

By CARLA HUTSON

Copyright 2025 By CARLA HUTSON. All rights reserved.

No part of this book may be reproduced in any form or by any electronic or mechanical means, including information storage and retrieval systems, without written permission from the author, except for the use of brief quotations in a book review.

Table of Contents

Introduction 6

Cheese Basics 11

How to Build a Cheese Board 20

Pairings for Cheese Boards 25

Themed Cheese Boards 35

Advanced Tips 62

*** Recipe *** 74

Floral Spring Cheese Board 75

Fresh Herb Cheese Board 77

Citrus Delight Cheese Board 78

Garden Veggie Cheese Board 79

Sweet and Savory Spring Cheese Board 80

Tropical Summer Cheese Board 81

Cozy Winter Cheese Board 83

Harvest Fall Cheese Board 85

Elegant Sparkle Cheese Board 87

Midnight Celebration Cheese Board 88

Golden Hour Cheese Board 89

Festive Countdown Cheese Board 90

Decadent New Year's Cheese Board 91

Romantic Red Cheese Board 92

Heartfelt Cheese Board 93

Sweet & Savory Love Board 94

Blush Pink Cheese Board 95

Decadent Chocolate & Cheese Board 96

Spooky Charcuterie Cheese Board 97

Pumpkin Patch Cheese Board 99

Graveyard Cheese Board	100
Witch's Cauldron Cheese Board	101
Monster Mash Cheese Board	102
Holiday Wreath Cheese Board	103
Snowy Christmas Cheese Board	104
Christmas Tree Cheese Board	105
Candy Cane Cheese Board	106
Warm & Cozy Christmas Cheese Board	107
Harvest Feast Cheese Board	108
Turkey Day Cheese Board	109
Cornucopia Cheese Board	110
Thankful Gathering Cheese Board	111
Autumn Colors Cheese Board	112
Classic Keto Cheese Board	113
Mediterranean Keto Cheese Board	114
Spicy Keto Cheese Board	115
Keto Charcuterie Cheese Board	116
Keto Sweet & Savory Cheese Board	117
Festive Vegan Cheese Board	118
Mediterranean Vegan Cheese Board	119
Spicy Vegan Cheese Board	120
Sweet & Savory Vegan Cheese Board	121
Holiday Vegan Cheese Board	122
Classic Gluten-Free Cheese Board	123
Mediterranean Gluten-Free Cheese Board	124
Autumn Harvest Gluten-Free Cheese Board	125
Spicy Gluten-Free Cheese Board	126
Sweet & Savory Gluten-Free Cheese Board	127

Classic Low-Lactose Cheese Board 128
Mediterranean Low-Lactose Cheese Board 129
Sweet & Savory Low-Lactose Cheese Board 130
Low-Lactose Spicy Cheese Board 131
Low-Lactose Holiday Cheese Board 132
Classic Nut-Free Cheese Board 133
Mediterranean Nut-Free Cheese Board 134
Fruit-Focused Nut-Free Cheese Board 135
Spicy Nut-Free Cheese Board 136
Holiday Nut-Free Cheese Board 137

Introduction

What Are Cheese Boards?

Cheese boards, also known as charcuterie boards or grazing boards (when paired with meats and other accompaniments), are thoughtfully arranged platters that showcase a variety of cheeses, complemented by an assortment of foods designed to enhance the experience. They combine elements of flavor, texture, and presentation to create a delicious and visually appealing centerpiece for any gathering.

At their simplest, cheese boards include a selection of cheeses paired with crackers or bread. However, they can be as elaborate as you like, incorporating a wide array of accompaniments, such as fresh and dried fruits, nuts, cured meats, spreads, pickles, and even decorative garnishes like herbs or edible flowers. The idea is to create a balance of flavors—sweet, savory, salty, tangy—and textures, from creamy to crunchy, in a way that excites the palate and invites exploration.

Cheese boards are highly versatile, making them perfect for any occasion. They can be small and simple, designed for a quiet evening at home, or expansive and themed, serving as the star attraction at parties, weddings, or holiday gatherings. Their charm lies in their adaptability, as they can cater to a variety of dietary preferences, seasonal ingredients, and creative presentation styles.

More than just food, cheese boards are a form of edible art. Arranging cheeses and accompaniments in an aesthetically pleasing way transforms the board into a show-stopping centerpiece that invites conversation and indulgence. Whether you're assembling a classic French-inspired board, a holiday-themed spread, or a colorful mix of seasonal flavors, cheese boards offer endless possibilities to delight your guests and elevate any gathering.

In essence, a cheese board is more than a meal—it's an experience. It encourages sharing, experimenting, and savoring each bite, bringing people together to enjoy the simple pleasures of good food and good company.

Essential Tools and Equipment

Creating the perfect cheese board requires not only delicious ingredients but also the right tools and equipment to prepare, display, and serve your masterpiece.

1. The Cheese Board

- **Material:** Choose from wood, marble, slate, or bamboo. Each material has its own aesthetic and functional qualities.
    - Wood: Classic and warm, great for rustic or traditional presentations.
    - Marble/Slate: Elegant and modern, these surfaces also keep cheeses cool.
- **Size and Shape:** Select a board that fits your guest count and desired layout. Round, rectangular, or irregularly shaped boards all work well.

2. Cheese Knives

Different types of knives are designed to handle various cheeses.

- Cheese Cleaver: For cutting firm and hard cheeses like cheddar or Parmesan.
- Cheese Spreader: For spreading soft cheeses like Brie or goat cheese.
- Soft Cheese Knife: For cutting creamy cheeses without sticking.
- Parmesan Knife: For breaking chunks from aged cheeses.
- Universal Cheese Knife: A versatile option for general use.

3. Small Bowls and Dishes

- Use small bowls or ramekins to hold dips, spreads, honey, olives, or nuts. These keep wet or sticky items separate from the dry elements and add visual interest to the board.

4. Tongs and Forks

- Mini Tongs or Forks: Ideal for picking up small items like grapes, pickles, or charcuterie slices without making a mess.
- Cheese Forks: Help guests pick up slices of harder cheeses.

5. Serving Utensils

- Spreaders: For butter, pâté, or spreads.
- Small Spoons: For honey, jams, or chutneys.

6. Cutting Board

- A separate cutting board is useful for slicing cheeses and accompaniments before assembling the main cheese board.

7. Decorative Elements

- Labels or Tags: Small signs to identify each cheese or accompaniment, especially helpful for guests unfamiliar with the selections.
- Edible Garnishes: Use herbs, flowers, or citrus slices to add flair.

8. Crackers and Bread Containers

- Baskets, small trays, or ramekins can hold crackers and slices of bread to keep them neat and accessible.

9. Serving Platter (Optional)

- For larger gatherings, a tiered serving platter or additional trays can expand your cheese board layout.

10. Chill Tools (Optional)

If you're serving cheeses outdoors or in warmer conditions:

- Marble Board or Chilled Plate: Helps keep cheeses cool.
- Ice Packs or Cooling Mats: Place under the board or bowls to maintain freshness.

Tools for Creativity

- Cheese Markers: Stylish labels to distinguish the cheeses.
- Slate Pencils or Chalk: Write directly on slate boards for a personalized touch.
- Food Tweezers: For precise placement of garnishes and smaller items.

Cheese Basics

Types of Cheese

Cheese is one of the most diverse and versatile foods, with hundreds of varieties made from cow, goat, sheep, or even buffalo milk. Each type of cheese has a unique texture, flavor profile, and pairing potential. Here's an overview of the main types of cheese:

1. Fresh Cheeses

Characteristics:

- Soft, creamy, and unripened.
- High moisture content and mild flavor.
- Best consumed shortly after production.

Examples:

- Mozzarella: Smooth and stretchy, often used in Italian dishes.
- Ricotta: Light, fluffy, and slightly sweet, perfect for both savory and sweet recipes.
- Cream Cheese: Soft and tangy, ideal for spreads and baking.
- Chevre (Goat Cheese): Tangy and creamy, often rolled in herbs or spices.

Pairings: Fresh fruits, honey, crusty bread, and light white wines.

2. Soft-Ripened Cheeses

Characteristics:

- Soft and creamy with a white, edible rind.
- Ripened from the outside in, becoming creamier as they age.

Examples:

- Brie: Buttery and earthy, with a gooey interior.

- Camembert: Similar to Brie but with a stronger, more rustic flavor.

Pairings: Crackers, figs, cured meats, and sparkling wines.

3. Semi-Soft Cheeses

Characteristics:

- Smooth, sliceable texture with mild to bold flavors.
- Often has a waxed or edible rind.

Examples:

- Gouda: Nutty and caramel-like, available in young or aged varieties.
- Havarti: Buttery and mild, often infused with herbs or spices.
- Munster: Creamy and slightly tangy, with an orange rind.

Pairings: Apples, nuts, light red wines, or craft beers.

4. Semi-Hard Cheeses

Characteristics:

- Firm texture but still easy to slice or grate.
- Balanced flavors, ranging from mild to sharp.

Examples:

- Cheddar: Aged varieties range from mild to sharp, with crumbly textures.
- Gruyère: Nutty and slightly sweet, perfect for melting.

- Provolone: Mild and slightly tangy, popular in sandwiches.

Pairings: Grapes, mustard, crusty bread, and medium-bodied wines.

5. **Hard Cheeses**

Characteristics:

- Low moisture content, dense, and crumbly texture.
- Aged for extended periods, resulting in concentrated flavors.

Examples:

- Parmesan (Parmigiano-Reggiano): Savory, nutty, and ideal for grating.
- Pecorino Romano: Made from sheep's milk, with a salty and sharp flavor.
- Asiago: Ranges from smooth and mild (young) to crumbly and sharp (aged).

Pairings: Nuts, olives, balsamic vinegar, and bold red wines.

6. **Blue Cheeses**

Characteristics:

- Veined with blue or green mold, giving a pungent aroma and bold flavor.
- Creamy to crumbly textures, depending on the variety.

Examples:

- Gorgonzola: Soft and tangy, ranging from mild to sharp.
- Roquefort: Made from sheep's milk, with a salty and robust taste.
- Stilton: Firm, creamy, and less salty than other blue cheeses.

Pairings: Pears, honey, walnuts, and dessert wines like Port.

7. Washed-Rind Cheeses

Characteristics:

- Washed with brine or alcohol during aging, creating a sticky, orange rind.
- Bold, funky aromas with creamy or semi-soft interiors.

Examples:

- Taleggio: Tangy, fruity, and creamy with a mild funk.
- Epoisses: Strong and aromatic with a rich, custardy interior.

Pairings: Crusty bread, pickles, and robust wines or beers.

8. Processed Cheeses

Characteristics:

- Made by blending cheeses with additional ingredients for smooth consistency.
- Often mild and shelf-stable.

Examples:

- American Cheese: Smooth, creamy, and popular in sandwiches.
- Cheese Spreads: Spreadable and often flavored with herbs or spices.

Pairings: Casual snacks, crackers, or burgers.

How to Select Cheese

Selecting the perfect cheeses for your board or recipe is an art that blends personal taste, occasion, and pairing possibilities. Whether you're preparing a simple cheese plate for a quiet night or an elaborate spread for a celebration, these tips will help you choose wisely.

1. Balance of Textures and Flavors

A great cheese selection includes a variety of textures and flavors to keep things interesting. Aim for diversity:

- Textures: Include soft (Brie, goat cheese), semi-soft (Havarti, Gouda), and hard or crumbly cheeses (Parmesan, aged Cheddar).
- Flavors: Mix mild cheeses (Mozzarella, Ricotta) with bold ones (blue cheese, aged Gruyère) for a dynamic range.
- Milk Types: Incorporate cheeses made from cow, goat, and sheep milk to introduce subtle differences in taste and texture.

2. **Consider the Occasion**

   - Casual Gatherings: Opt for approachable and crowd-pleasing cheeses like Cheddar, Gouda, and Brie.
   - Formal Events: Elevate the selection with artisanal or aged cheeses like Camembert, Manchego, or Roquefort.
   - Themed Boards: Choose cheeses that match the theme, such as French cheeses (Brie, Comté, Roquefort) for a Parisian-inspired board or Italian varieties (Mozzarella, Taleggio, Parmesan) for an Italian spread.

3. **Seasonal Selection**

Cheese, like produce, has seasons. Select cheeses that are at their peak flavor:

   - Spring: Fresh cheeses like goat cheese and Ricotta.
   - Summer: Light, creamy cheeses like Mozzarella and Burrata.
   - Fall: Aged and nutty cheeses like Gruyère, aged Cheddar, or Gouda.
   - Winter: Bold, rich flavors like blue cheese or washed-rind varieties.

4. **Know Your Audience**

   - For Beginners: Choose mild and familiar cheeses like Colby, Monterey Jack, or Brie.
   - For Adventurous Guests: Include bold, funky cheeses like Epoisses, Stilton, or aged Gruyère.
   - Dietary Preferences: Offer lactose-free, vegan, or nut-based cheeses if needed.

5. **Pairing Potential**

Consider what you'll be serving alongside the cheese:

- Fruits and Nuts: Mild cheeses like Brie pair well with sweet fruits and honey, while sharp or tangy cheeses like blue cheese complement savory or salty flavors.
- Wine and Beer: Match wine and beer to your cheeses. For example, aged Cheddar pairs with full-bodied reds, and creamy cheeses like Brie pair with sparkling wines.
- Spreads and Crackers: Choose cheeses that balance well with your selection of bread, crackers, and dips.

6. Portion Planning

When assembling a cheese board, plan the right amount of cheese per person:

- Appetizers: 1–2 ounces per person.
- Main Course: 3–4 ounces per person.
- Tasting or Sampling: Smaller portions of a variety of cheeses to encourage exploration.

7. Buy Fresh and Local When Possible

- Artisanal Cheese Shops: These often have knowledgeable staff who can guide your choices and offer samples.
- Farmers' Markets: A great source for local, fresh, and seasonal cheeses.
- Supermarkets: Look for quality brands and small-batch options in the specialty cheese section.

8. Experiment and Learn

Cheese selection can be a fun journey. Try new cheeses regularly, and note what you and your guests enjoy. Over time, you'll develop a deeper understanding of your preferences and pairing combinations.

How to Build a Cheese Board

Building a cheese board is both an art and a science—it's about creating a beautiful presentation while balancing flavors, textures, and pairings to delight your guests.

1. Choose Your Board

- Material: Use wood, marble, slate, or a large platter. Each material offers a different aesthetic and functionality.
- Size: Select a board large enough to hold your cheeses and accompaniments without overcrowding. For larger gatherings, you can use multiple boards or tiered trays.

2. Select the Cheeses

Aim for variety and balance:

- Include 3 to 5 types of cheese to avoid overwhelming your guests.
- Pick a mix of textures:
  - Soft and creamy: Brie, goat cheese.
  - Semi-soft: Havarti, Gouda.
  - Firm and aged: Cheddar, Parmesan.
  - Bold: Blue cheese, Roquefort.
- Choose cheeses made from different milk types (cow, goat, sheep) for diversity in flavor.

Portion Tip: Plan for 1–2 ounces of cheese per person if served as an appetizer, or 3–4 ounces if it's the main attraction.

3. Add Accompaniments

Complement your cheeses with a mix of sweet, savory, and crunchy options:

- Crackers and Bread: Offer a variety, such as baguette slices, water crackers, and seeded crisps.

- Fruits: Use fresh fruits like grapes, apple slices, figs, or pears, and dried options like apricots, dates, or cranberries.
- Nuts: Almonds, walnuts, and pecans add crunch and richness.
- Spreads: Include honey, fig jam, chutney, or fruit preserves for sweetness.
- Pickled Items: Olives, cornichons, or pickled onions add a tangy contrast.
- Charcuterie (Optional): Salami, prosciutto, or other cured meats pair wonderfully with cheeses.

4. Arrange the Cheeses

- Start with the Cheese: Place the cheeses on the board first, spacing them out to create structure.
  - Leave room for cutting and spreading.
  - Pre-slice or crumble hard cheeses for easy serving.
- Arrange the cheeses in an aesthetically pleasing way, such as grouping them by shape or type.

5. Place Accompaniments

- Fill in the Gaps: Arrange accompaniments around the cheeses.
  - Place fruits and nuts in clusters for visual appeal.
  - Use small bowls for spreads, dips, or wet items like olives.
- Layer for Texture: Add height with stacks of crackers or piles of nuts.

- Balance the Colors: Spread out vibrant fruits and garnishes to create a visually appealing board.

6. Add Final Touches

- Garnish: Use fresh herbs (like rosemary or thyme) or edible flowers for decoration.
- Labels: Add cheese markers or small tags to identify each cheese, especially if your guests are unfamiliar with them.

7. Serve and Enjoy

- Room Temperature: Let the cheese sit out for 30–60 minutes before serving to allow the flavors to develop.
- Serving Tools: Provide the appropriate knives, forks, or spreaders for each type of cheese. Mini tongs or toothpicks can make it easier for guests to grab accompaniments.

8. Themed Boards (Optional)

For special occasions, you can create themed cheese boards, such as:

- Seasonal: Incorporate seasonal fruits and flavors (e.g., apples and nuts for fall).
- Regional: Showcase cheeses and accompaniments from a specific country or area.

- Holiday: Add festive touches like cranberry chutney or decorative garnishes for Christmas or Thanksgiving.

Pairings for Cheese Boards

Pairings elevate a cheese board from good to unforgettable by enhancing the flavors and textures of the cheeses. Thoughtfully chosen accompaniments can bring out the best in every bite.

1. **Fruits**

Fruits add natural sweetness and acidity, providing contrast to salty, creamy, or sharp cheeses.

Fresh Fruits:

- Grapes: Versatile and classic, pairing well with most cheeses, especially Brie, Cheddar, and Gouda.
- Apples: Crisp and tart, complementing sharp Cheddar and blue cheese.
- Pears: Sweet and juicy, ideal with creamy Brie, goat cheese, and blue cheeses.
- Figs: Fresh figs pair beautifully with Brie and Camembert, while dried figs work well with aged cheeses like Parmesan.
- Berries: Strawberries, raspberries, and blackberries are great with soft cheeses like Ricotta and goat cheese.

Dried Fruits:

- Apricots: Their sweetness pairs wonderfully with salty or tangy cheeses like blue cheese.
- Dates: Rich and sticky, a perfect contrast for aged or sharp cheeses like Manchego or Gouda.
- Cranberries: Add tartness to creamy cheeses like Brie or Havarti.

2. **Nuts**

Nuts provide crunch and earthy flavors that enhance the texture of creamy or crumbly cheeses.

- Almonds: Pair well with aged Gouda, Manchego, and Parmesan.
- Walnuts: Complement blue cheese, Brie, and goat cheese with their slightly bitter notes.
- Pecans: Sweet and buttery, they pair nicely with creamy cheeses like Brie or Havarti.
- Hazelnuts: Their nutty flavor is a great match for Gruyère and Cheddar.
- Candied Nuts: Add sweetness and crunch, ideal for pairing with bold cheeses like blue cheese or aged Cheddar.

3. **Spreads and Condiments**

Sweet and tangy spreads enhance the flavor of almost any cheese by adding balance.

- Honey: A classic pairing for salty cheeses like blue cheese, goat cheese, and Parmesan.
- Jams and Preserves:
    - Fig jam: Perfect for Brie, Camembert, and goat cheese.
    - Apricot jam: A great match for Gouda, Havarti, or blue cheese.
    - Raspberry or cherry preserves: Pair well with creamy cheeses like Brie or Mascarpone.

- Chutneys: Sweet and savory chutneys, such as mango or onion chutney, pair well with sharp Cheddar or aged Gouda.
- Mustards: Whole-grain or Dijon mustard complements tangy cheeses like Gruyère or aged Cheddar.

4. Crackers and Bread

The base for serving cheese, crackers and bread provide texture and a neutral flavor to highlight the cheese.

Crackers:

- Water crackers: Light and neutral, allowing the cheese to shine.
- Seeded crackers: Add texture and pair well with creamy cheeses.
- Herb-infused crackers: Complement herbed cheeses or mild varieties.

Bread:

- Baguette slices: Perfect for spreading soft cheeses like Brie or goat cheese.
- Rustic sourdough: Pairs well with aged and bold cheeses like Gruyère or Cheddar.
- Crostini: Toasted bread provides crunch and pairs with any cheese and spread.

5. Pickled and Briny Items

The tanginess of pickled and briny foods cuts through the richness of cheese, adding balance and a punch of flavor.

- Olives: Salty and briny, they pair well with feta, Manchego, and Parmigiano-Reggiano.
- Cornichons: Their tartness complements rich and creamy cheeses like Brie or blue cheese.
- Pickled Vegetables: Carrots, onions, or asparagus add crunch and tang, great with semi-soft cheeses like Havarti or Gouda.

6. Charcuterie

Cured meats are a classic addition to cheese boards, offering savory, smoky, or spicy flavors.

- Salami: Pairs well with sharp or aged cheeses like Cheddar and Parmesan.
- Prosciutto: Its delicate flavor is perfect with creamy cheeses like Mozzarella, Brie, or Burrata.
- Chorizo: Spicy and bold, pairs with aged cheeses like Manchego or Gruyère.
- Soppressata: Complements tangy and bold cheeses like blue cheese or aged Gouda.

7. **Beverages**

Pairing the right drinks with your cheese board enhances the overall tasting experience.

Wine:

- Red: Full-bodied wines like Cabernet Sauvignon pair with aged Cheddar or Gruyère. Light reds like Pinot Noir are perfect for Brie or Camembert.
- White: Crisp whites like Sauvignon Blanc or Chardonnay complement goat cheese and Brie.
- Sparkling: Champagne or Prosecco pairs with creamy cheeses and salty accompaniments.

Beer:

- Light beers like pilsners pair well with mild cheeses like Havarti.

- IPAs complement bold cheeses like blue cheese.
- Stouts pair beautifully with nutty, aged cheeses like Gouda or Cheddar.

Non-Alcoholic Options:

- Sparkling water or cider pairs well with any cheese.
- Herbal teas complement mild cheeses, while bold teas pair with aged varieties.

8. Herbs and Garnishes

- Fresh herbs like rosemary, thyme, or basil add a fragrant touch and visual appeal.
- Edible flowers can elevate the presentation and add delicate flavors to the board.

Pairing Tips:

- Contrast or Complement: Pair cheese with accompaniments that either contrast its flavor (e.g., salty blue cheese with sweet honey) or complement it (e.g., nutty Gruyère with toasted almonds).
- Experiment: Don't be afraid to try unexpected pairings—some of the most delightful combinations come from experimentation.
- Keep It Balanced: Ensure your cheese board has a mix of sweet, salty, tangy, and savory elements for a well-rounded experience.

Themed Cheese Boards

Seasonal Boards

1. Spring Cheese Board

Spring is a season of freshness, lightness, and renewal. Think young cheeses, vibrant colors, and fresh herbs.

Cheeses:

- Fresh Goat Cheese: Creamy and tangy, perfect for spring flavors.
- Brie: Soft and mild, with a creamy texture that pairs well with sweet and floral accompaniments.
- Young Gouda: Smooth and slightly nutty, not overpowering.
- Feta: Salty and crumbly, ideal for balancing sweet fruits or vegetables.

Accompaniments:

- Fruits: Fresh strawberries, apricots, and pears.
- Vegetables: Sliced radishes, sugar snap peas, or cucumber ribbons.
- Herbs: Fresh mint, basil, or thyme sprigs.
- Spreads: Honey with edible flowers, lemon curd, or light fruit jams (like apricot or raspberry).
- Nuts: Toasted almonds or pistachios for crunch.
- Crackers/Bread: Light, airy crackers or sliced baguette.

Decorative Touches:

- Edible flowers (like pansies or nasturtiums) for a pop of color.
- Fresh herbs for greenery.

Beverage Pairings:

- Sauvignon Blanc, rosé, or sparkling water infused with citrus and herbs.

2. Summer Cheese Board

Summer is all about vibrant, juicy produce and light, creamy cheeses. Opt for refreshing, easy-to-eat items perfect for warm-weather gatherings.

Cheeses:

- Mozzarella/Burrata: Creamy and mild, perfect with summer tomatoes.
- Havarti: Buttery and soft, with a smooth texture.
- Manchego: A semi-firm Spanish cheese with a slightly nutty flavor.
- Ricotta: Light and fluffy, ideal for spreading.

Accompaniments:

- Fruits: Watermelon slices, fresh peaches, cherries, and figs.
- Vegetables: Cherry tomatoes, bell pepper slices, or cucumber rounds.
- Spreads: Basil pesto, honey, or balsamic glaze.
- Nuts: Lightly salted Marcona almonds or cashews.
- Crackers/Bread: Crostini or herb flatbreads.

Decorative Touches:

- Basil leaves, fresh lavender, or rosemary sprigs.

Beverage Pairings:

- Rosé wine, Prosecco, or citrusy sangria.

3. Fall Cheese Board

Fall is the season of warmth, comfort, and earthy flavors. Incorporate rich cheeses, warm spices, and seasonal produce to capture the essence of autumn.

Cheeses:

- Aged Cheddar: Sharp and crumbly, a fall favorite.
- Gruyère: Nutty and slightly sweet, perfect for pairing with fall accompaniments.
- Blue Cheese (Gorgonzola or Stilton): Bold and tangy, balances sweet fall fruits.
- Goat Cheese (Rolled in Cranberries or Herbs): Creamy with a seasonal touch.

Accompaniments:

- Fruits: Sliced apples, pears, and dried figs.
- Vegetables: Roasted butternut squash cubes or spiced pumpkin wedges.
- Spreads: Apple butter, fig jam, or spiced honey.
- Nuts: Candied pecans, walnuts, or hazelnuts.
- Crackers/Bread: Multigrain crackers, sourdough slices, or seeded crisps.

Decorative Touches:

- Cinnamon sticks, star anise, or mini pumpkins.
- Autumn leaves (ensure they're clean and food-safe).

Beverage Pairings:

- Full-bodied red wines (Cabernet Sauvignon), spiced cider, or pumpkin ale.

4. Winter Cheese Board

Winter is the time for bold, rich flavors and festive elements. Focus on hearty cheeses, dried fruits, and warming spices.

Cheeses:

- Camembert or Brie (Baked): Creamy and decadent, often topped with nuts or honey.
- Aged Gouda: Caramel-like sweetness and firm texture.
- Parmesan (Parmigiano-Reggiano): Savory and nutty, adds a robust element.
- Blue Cheese (Roquefort or Stilton): Bold and creamy, perfect for winter pairings.

Accompaniments:

- Fruits: Pomegranate seeds, dried cranberries, and dates.
- Vegetables: Roasted root vegetables or pickled red onions.
- Spreads: Fig preserves, cranberry chutney, or honey infused with cinnamon.
- Nuts: Candied pecans, spiced almonds, or roasted chestnuts.

- Crackers/Bread: Rye bread, crispbread, or rosemary crackers.

Decorative Touches:

- Sprigs of rosemary, holly leaves (non-edible), or sugared cranberries for a festive touch.

Beverage Pairings:

- Port wine, mulled wine, or spiced hot cider.

Regional Boards

Themed regional cheese boards highlight the unique flavors, cheeses, and accompaniments of a specific country or region. They celebrate local culinary traditions and allow your guests to experience the authentic taste of a destination.

1. French Cheese Board

France is famous for its diverse and exquisite cheeses, offering a mix of creamy, nutty, and bold flavors.

Cheeses:

- Brie: Soft, creamy, and buttery.
- Camembert: Similar to Brie but slightly earthier.
- Roquefort: A bold blue cheese made from sheep's milk.
- Comté: A nutty and slightly sweet hard cheese.
- Chèvre: Tangy, fresh goat cheese.

Accompaniments:

- Fruits: Fresh figs, grapes, or sliced pears.
- Bread: Crusty French baguette and pain d'épi.
- Spreads: Fig jam, apricot preserves, or honey.
- Nuts: Walnuts or almonds.
- Other: Cornichons, Dijon mustard.

Decorative Touches:

- Fresh thyme or lavender sprigs for an authentic French feel.

Beverage Pairings:

- Champagne, Bordeaux, or a crisp Sauvignon Blanc.

2. Italian Cheese Board

Italian boards focus on bold, rich flavors and Mediterranean accompaniments.

Cheeses:

- Parmigiano-Reggiano: Aged and nutty with a crumbly texture.
- Pecorino Romano: Salty and sharp, made from sheep's milk.
- Taleggio: A creamy and tangy washed-rind cheese.
- Mozzarella or Burrata: Soft, fresh, and delicate.

Accompaniments:

- Fruits: Fresh figs, grapes, and dried apricots.
- Vegetables: Marinated artichokes, roasted red peppers, and olives.

- Bread: Focaccia, crostini, or grissini breadsticks.
- Spreads: Tomato bruschetta or balsamic glaze.
- Meats: Prosciutto, salami, or coppa.

Decorative Touches:

- Fresh basil leaves or rosemary sprigs.

Beverage Pairings:

- Chianti, Prosecco, or a fruity Pinot Grigio.

3. Spanish Cheese Board

Spanish cheese boards feature bold, aged cheeses and flavorful Mediterranean accompaniments.

Cheeses:

- Manchego: A nutty and firm sheep's milk cheese.
- Idiazabal: Smoky and firm, made from sheep's milk.
- Cabrales: A pungent and bold blue cheese.
- Mahón: A semi-soft, slightly tangy cow's milk cheese.

Accompaniments:

- Fruits: Quince paste (membrillo), oranges, or dates.
- Nuts: Marcona almonds, lightly salted.
- Bread: Rustic bread or olive oil crackers.
- Meats: Jamón serrano, chorizo, or lomo.
- Other: Olives, roasted piquillo peppers.

Decorative Touches:

- Olive branches or sprigs of thyme.

Beverage Pairings:

- Rioja, sherry, or sparkling cava.

4. British Cheese Board

The UK boasts a rich tradition of artisanal cheeses with bold flavors and crumbly textures.

Cheeses:

- Stilton: A creamy and pungent blue cheese.
- Cheddar: Aged and sharp with a crumbly texture.
- Double Gloucester: Rich and buttery.
- Wensleydale: Mild and crumbly, often paired with cranberries.

Accompaniments:

- Fruits: Apples, pears, and grapes.
- Bread/Crackers: Digestive biscuits or oatcakes.
- Spreads: Chutney, onion marmalade, or honey.
- Nuts: Walnuts or pecans.

Decorative Touches:

- Sprigs of rosemary or small bundles of wheat.

Beverage Pairings:

- Port, cider, or a malty English ale.

5. Swiss Cheese Board

Swiss boards showcase creamy and nutty alpine-style cheeses, perfect for pairing with hearty accompaniments.

Cheeses:

- Gruyère: Nutty and slightly sweet.
- Emmental: Mild and slightly tangy with signature holes.
- Appenzeller: Creamy and spicy, with a washed rind.
- Tête de Moine: Shaved into delicate rosettes for an elegant touch.

Accompaniments:

- Fruits: Apples, grapes, and dried apricots.
- Bread: Sliced rye bread or pretzel rolls.
- Spreads: Mustard or fruit preserves.
- Other: Cornichons, pickled pearl onions.

Decorative Touches:

- Fresh dill or edible alpine flowers.

Beverage Pairings:

- Dry white wine (Chasselas), Riesling, or a crisp lager.

6. American Artisanal Cheese Board

Showcasing the best of small-batch, artisanal cheeses from across the U.S., this board celebrates local flavors and creativity.

Cheeses:

- Aged Cheddar (Vermont): Sharp and crumbly.

- Point Reyes Blue (California): Bold and creamy blue cheese.
- Cypress Grove Humboldt Fog (California): A tangy goat cheese with a beautiful ash layer.
- Rogue River Blue (Oregon): A unique, smoky blue cheese wrapped in grape leaves.

Accompaniments:

- Fruits: Seasonal fruits like apples, pears, or berries.
- Nuts: Spiced pecans or smoked almonds.
- Bread: Sourdough slices or wheat crackers.
- Spreads: Apple butter, honey, or bourbon-infused jams.

Decorative Touches:

- Seasonal flowers or rustic wooden boards.

Beverage Pairings:

- Craft beers, cider, or small-batch bourbon.

7. Middle Eastern Cheese Board

Middle Eastern boards highlight fresh, tangy cheeses and vibrant accompaniments.

Cheeses:

- Feta: Salty and crumbly, often marinated in olive oil with herbs.
- Halloumi: A grillable, semi-firm cheese.
- Labneh: Creamy and tangy, served with olive oil and za'atar.

Accompaniments:

- Fruits: Pomegranate seeds, dried figs, and apricots.
- Vegetables: Sliced cucumber, cherry tomatoes, or roasted eggplant.
- Bread: Pita bread or lavash.
- Spreads: Hummus, baba ghanoush, or muhammara (roasted red pepper dip).
- Nuts: Pistachios or almonds.

Decorative Touches:

- Sprinkles of za'atar or sumac for a colorful touch.

Beverage Pairings:

- Mint tea, dry white wine, or sparkling water with lime.

Holiday Boards

Holiday-themed cheese boards bring festive flavors, colors, and decorations to your table, making them the perfect centerpiece for seasonal celebrations. Each board reflects the spirit of the holiday through carefully selected cheeses, accompaniments, and creative presentation.

1. Christmas Cheese Board

A Christmas board should be festive and indulgent, showcasing bold flavors, vibrant colors, and seasonal touches.

Cheeses:

- Brie: Creamy and crowd-pleasing; bake it with cranberries for extra flair.
- Blue Cheese: Bold and tangy, perfect with sweet holiday accompaniments.

- Aged Cheddar: Sharp and nutty, a great contrast to sweet items.
- Gruyère: Smooth and slightly sweet, ideal for melting or pairing.

Accompaniments:

- Fruits: Pomegranate seeds, red grapes, and dried cranberries.
- Nuts: Candied pecans, spiced almonds, or walnuts.
- Spreads: Cranberry chutney, fig jam, or honey.
- Crackers/Bread: Rosemary crackers, baguette slices, or seeded crisps.

Decorative Touches:

- Sprigs of rosemary, sugared cranberries, or mini ornaments.

Beverage Pairings:

- Mulled wine, spiced cider, or Champagne.

2. New Year's Eve Cheese Board

A New Year's Eve board should be elegant and celebratory, perfect for pairing with sparkling wines and cocktails.

Cheeses:

- Camembert: Soft and creamy with a subtle, earthy flavor.
- Aged Gouda: Rich and caramel-like for an indulgent touch.
- Goat Cheese: Fresh and tangy; roll it in herbs or edible glitter for sparkle.

- Parmigiano-Reggiano: Savory and crumbly, ideal for nibbling.

Accompaniments:

- Fruits: Dried apricots, golden raisins, and fresh grapes.
- Nuts: Honey-roasted almonds or spiced cashews.
- Spreads: Honey infused with truffle or gold flakes, champagne jelly.
- Crackers/Bread: Lavash crisps, water crackers, or thin breadsticks.

Decorative Touches:

- Edible gold leaf, metallic sprinkles, or star-shaped crackers.

Beverage Pairings:

- Champagne, sparkling rosé, or Prosecco.

3. Valentine's Day Cheese Board

Valentine's Day boards should be romantic, featuring rich, creamy cheeses and sweet, heart-shaped accents.

Cheeses:

- Heart-Shaped Brie: Soft and creamy, perfect for a romantic touch.
- Triple Cream Cheese: Decadent and buttery.
- Goat Cheese: Fresh and tangy; roll it in pink peppercorns or dried rose petals.
- Aged Cheddar: Sharp and robust to balance sweet flavors.

Accompaniments:

- Fruits: Strawberries, raspberries, cherries, and red grapes.
- Chocolate: Dark chocolate chunks or chocolate-covered almonds.
- Spreads: Raspberry jam, honey, or chocolate hazelnut spread.
- Crackers/Bread: Heart-shaped crackers or chocolate wafers.

Decorative Touches:

- Edible flowers, rose petals, or heart-shaped cutouts from cheese or fruit.

Beverage Pairings:

- Rosé wine, Champagne, or a chocolate-infused cocktail.

4. Easter Cheese Board

Easter boards should be light, colorful, and fresh, celebrating springtime flavors.

Cheeses:

- Fresh Goat Cheese: Tangy and creamy, perfect with spring flavors.
- Ricotta: Light and fluffy for spreading.
- Young Gouda: Smooth and mild.
- Burrata: Soft and creamy, ideal for pairing with fresh veggies.

Accompaniments:

- Fruits: Fresh berries, apricots, and kiwi slices.
- Vegetables: Baby carrots, radishes, and snap peas.
- Spreads: Lemon curd, honey, or light fruit preserves.
- Nuts: Pistachios or lightly salted almonds.
- Crackers/Bread: Multigrain crackers or crostini.

Decorative Touches:

- Edible flowers, pastel candies, or bunny-shaped crackers.

Beverage Pairings:

- Light white wine, sparkling water with citrus, or mimosas.

5. Halloween Cheese Board

Halloween boards should be fun, spooky, and vibrant, with a mix of bold flavors and playful decorations.

Cheeses:

- Orange Cheddar: Bright and sharp, a festive choice.
- Blue Cheese: Bold and slightly eerie in appearance.
- Smoked Gouda: Smoky and savory, perfect for a Halloween vibe.
- Goat Cheese: Shape it into a ghost or roll it in black sesame seeds.

Accompaniments:

- Fruits: Blackberries, dried apricots, and red apple slices.
- Vegetables: Carrot sticks or roasted pumpkin wedges.
- Spreads: Blood-red jams (like cherry or raspberry).

- Nuts: Spiced pecans or pumpkin seeds.
- Crackers/Bread: Black crackers or charcoal-infused breadsticks.

Decorative Touches:

- Mini pumpkins, candy eyeballs, or plastic spiders (non-edible).

Beverage Pairings:

- Spiced cider, pumpkin ale, or dark red wine (like Malbec).

6. Thanksgiving Cheese Board

Thanksgiving boards should reflect the warmth and richness of the holiday, incorporating seasonal ingredients and bold flavors.

Cheeses:

- Aged Cheddar: Sharp and crumbly.
- Gruyère: Smooth and nutty, great for melting or pairing.
- Blue Cheese: Rich and tangy, perfect with sweet accompaniments.
- Goat Cheese (Rolled in Cranberries or Pecans): A festive, tangy option.

Accompaniments:

- Fruits: Sliced apples, pears, and dried figs.
- Nuts: Candied pecans or spiced walnuts.
- Spreads: Cranberry sauce, pumpkin butter, or honey.
- Crackers/Bread: Multigrain crackers, sourdough slices, or cornbread crisps.

Decorative Touches:

- Small gourds, cinnamon sticks, or rosemary sprigs.

Beverage Pairings:

- Full-bodied red wines (like Pinot Noir) or spiced cider.

Dietary Boards

Creating dietary-specific cheese boards ensures everyone can enjoy the spread, regardless of their dietary restrictions or preferences. Whether your guests are keto, vegan, gluten-free, or prefer low-lactose options.

1. Keto Cheese Board

A keto-friendly board focuses on low-carb, high-fat ingredients, making cheese the star of the show.

Cheeses:

- Aged Cheddar: High in fat and low in carbs, with sharp flavor.
- Blue Cheese: Bold and creamy, perfect for keto pairing.
- Gruyère: Smooth, nutty, and keto-friendly.
- Goat Cheese: Tangy and versatile.
- Parmesan: Savory and rich, ideal for snacking or grating.

Accompaniments:

- Proteins: Prosciutto, salami, or bacon-wrapped jalapeños.

- Low-Carb Vegetables: Cucumber slices, celery sticks, cherry tomatoes, or bell pepper strips.
- Nuts: Macadamia nuts, almonds, or walnuts (unsweetened).
- Spreads: Pesto, guacamole, or olive tapenade.
- Other: Olives, pickles, and small cheese crisps for added crunch.

Decorative Touches:

- Keto-friendly almond or seed-based crackers, Parmesan crisps, or pork rinds.

Beverage Pairings:

- Dry red wine, whiskey, or sparkling water.

2. Vegan Cheese Board

A vegan board features plant-based cheeses and dairy-free accompaniments while maintaining the classic cheese board appeal.

Cheeses:

- Cashew Brie: Smooth and creamy, mimicking traditional Brie.
- Almond Feta: Crumbly and tangy, great for pairing.
- Vegan Cheddar: Sharp and firm, made from coconut oil or cashews.
- Vegan Blue Cheese: Bold and tangy, crafted with cultured nut bases.

- Mozzarella-Style Cheese: Soft and mild, ideal for spreads or melting.

Accompaniments:

- Fruits: Fresh berries, apple slices, figs, and dried apricots.
- Vegetables: Carrot, Roasted red peppers, cucumber slices, and cherry tomatoes.
- Nuts: Toasted almonds, pistachios, or spiced cashews.
- Spreads: Hummus, baba ghanoush, or fruit preserves.
- Other: Marinated artichokes, olives, or pickled vegetables.

Decorative Touches:

- Gluten-free crackers, vegetable chips, or pita chips (dairy-free).

Beverage Pairings:

- Sparkling water, kombucha, or vegan-friendly wine.

3. Gluten-Free Cheese Board

A gluten-free board ensures that all components are free from wheat and gluten-containing ingredients.

Cheeses:

- All naturally gluten-free cheeses, such as:
- Aged Cheddar: Sharp and crumbly.
- Goat Cheese: Creamy and tangy.
- Gruyère: Nutty and smooth.
- Brie: Soft and mild.
- Parmesan: Hard and savory.

Accompaniments:

- Fruits: Grapes, apples, pears, and dried figs (ensure they are unsweetened and gluten-free).
- Vegetables: Carrot sticks, celery, cucumber slices, or cherry tomatoes.
- Nuts: Raw almonds, walnuts, or pecans.
- Spreads: Gluten-free fruit jams, honey, or chutneys.
- Other: Olives, cornichons, or roasted chickpeas.

Decorative Touches:

- Gluten-free crackers made from rice, almond flour, or seeds.
- Sliced sweet potatoes, rice cakes, or crispbread.

Beverage Pairings:

- Gluten-free beer, cider, or sparkling wine.

4. Low-Lactose Cheese Board

For those who are lactose-intolerant but enjoy cheese, this board includes low-lactose and lactose-free options.

Cheeses:

- Aged Cheeses (Low Lactose):
- Parmesan
- Aged Cheddar
- Gruyère
- Pecorino Romano
- Lactose-Free Cheeses: Many soft and hard cheeses now come in lactose-free varieties.

Accompaniments:

- Fruits: Fresh figs, grapes, and pears.
- Nuts: Walnuts, almonds, or pistachios.
- Spreads: Honey, fruit preserves, or mustard.
- Other: Olives, pickles, or marinated artichokes.

Decorative Touches:

- Gluten-free or seed-based crackers (ensure they are also lactose-free).

Beverage Pairings:

- Dry red or white wines, herbal teas, or sparkling water.

5. Paleo Cheese Board

A paleo board focuses on unprocessed, whole foods with no grains or refined sugar.

Cheeses:

- Some interpretations of the paleo diet exclude dairy, but many allow raw or minimally processed cheeses.
- Allowed Cheeses: Raw milk cheeses like aged Cheddar, Parmesan, or Pecorino.

Accompaniments:

- Fruits: Fresh berries, apple slices, and dried dates (unsweetened).
- Vegetables: Cucumber slices, cherry tomatoes, or bell pepper strips.
- Nuts: Walnuts, macadamia nuts, or almonds.
- Spreads: Almond butter, guacamole, or olive tapenade.

- Other: Olives, smoked salmon, or prosciutto (without added sugar).

Decorative Touches:

- Paleo-friendly crackers made from almond or coconut flour, or fresh vegetable slices.

Beverage Pairings:

- Dry wine or sparkling water with lime.

6. Nut-Free Cheese Board

A nut-free board eliminates all nuts and nut-based products, replacing them with seeds, fruits, and other safe alternatives.

Cheeses:

- Any Cheese: Ensure no nuts were used during processing or packaging.
- Examples: Brie, Havarti, Manchego, Gouda, or Cheddar.

Accompaniments:

- Fruits: Fresh grapes, apples, pears, and dried apricots (check for nut contamination).

- Vegetables: Celery sticks, cucumber rounds, or cherry tomatoes.
- Seeds: Roasted sunflower seeds, pumpkin seeds, or chia seed crisps.
- Spreads: Seed butters, fruit jams, or honey.
- Other: Olives, pickles, or marinated artichokes.

Decorative Touches:

- Seed-based crackers or rice cakes.

Beverage Pairings:

- Sparkling water, juice, or nut-free wines.

Advanced Tips

Tips for Common Cheese Board Challenges

Creating a cheese board is an enjoyable process, but even seasoned hosts can run into challenges. From keeping cheese fresh to ensuring the board is visually appealing, here are solutions to common problems you might encounter:

1. Preventing Cheese from Drying Out

Cheese can dry out quickly when exposed to air for extended periods, losing its texture and flavor.

Tips:

- Pre-Cut Larger Cheeses: Slice or cube hard cheeses like Parmesan or Cheddar just before serving to minimize exposure.
- Cover with Plastic Wrap: For soft or creamy cheeses, loosely cover the exposed side with plastic wrap until ready to serve.
- Keep It Cool: Use a marble or slate board that can be chilled to help maintain freshness during serving.
- Serve Smaller Portions: Place half the cheese on the board and replenish as needed to reduce the time it sits out.

2. Balancing Flavors and Textures

An unbalanced board may feel one-dimensional, with too many cheeses of the same flavor profile or texture.

Tips:

- Aim for Variety: Include at least one cheese from each category (soft, semi-soft, hard, and blue).
- Mix Flavors: Incorporate mild, tangy, nutty, and bold cheeses.
- Add Contrasting Accompaniments: Balance creamy cheeses with crunchy nuts, salty cheeses with sweet fruits, and bold cheeses with mild crackers.

3. Managing Overcrowded or Sparse Boards

An overcrowded board looks messy, while a sparse board may seem incomplete.

Tips for Avoiding Overcrowding:

- Plan the Layout First: Place cheeses first, then arrange accompaniments around them.
- Use Bowls or Small Dishes: Contain spreads, nuts, and small items in bowls to free up space.
- Limit the Selection: Stick to 3–5 types of cheese to avoid overwhelming the board.

Tips for Avoiding Sparse Boards:

- Fill Empty Spaces: Use fresh herbs, edible flowers, or extra nuts to fill gaps.
- Layer Items: Stack crackers or fruit slices to add volume.
- Use a Smaller Board: If you don't have enough items, a smaller board will naturally look fuller.

4. Preventing Cheese from Sticking

Soft cheeses can stick to knives, making it difficult to cut and serve neatly.

Tips:

- Use the Right Knife: Use soft cheese knives with holes in the blade to reduce sticking.
- Chill Soft Cheeses: Briefly refrigerate soft cheeses like Brie or Camembert before serving to firm them up slightly.
- Wipe Between Cuts: Keep a damp cloth nearby to wipe the knife clean between slices.

5. Keeping Cheese Fresh Outdoors

When serving cheese outdoors, heat and humidity can quickly spoil your board.

Tips:

- Use a Chilled Board: Serve on a marble or slate board that's been refrigerated beforehand.
- Serve in Batches: Keep half the board refrigerated and replenish as needed.
- Provide Shade: If outdoors, keep the board out of direct sunlight by using a canopy or umbrella.
- Use Ice Packs: Place ice packs under the board, concealed by a decorative cloth.

6. Making It Easy to Serve

Guests may struggle to cut hard cheeses or spread soft cheeses neatly.

Tips:

- Pre-Slice or Pre-Crumbly Cheeses: Cut hard cheeses into small wedges or chunks.
- Provide Spreading Tools: Include cheese spreaders or butter knives for soft cheeses.
- Label Cheeses: Add small tags or signs to identify each cheese so guests can choose without hesitation.

7. Pairing Accompaniments Correctly

Inappropriate pairings can overpower or clash with the cheese.

Tips:

- Know the Basics: Pair bold cheeses like blue cheese with sweet items (e.g., honey or figs) and mild cheeses like Brie with subtle flavors (e.g., almonds or apples).
- Provide a Range: Offer both sweet and savory accompaniments to suit all tastes.
- Test in Advance: If you're trying new pairings, sample them before serving to ensure they work well together.

8. Managing Strong-Smelling Cheeses

Bold cheeses like blue cheese or Limburger can overwhelm other flavors or offend sensitive noses.

Tips:

- Separate Strong-Smelling Cheeses: Place pungent cheeses away from milder varieties on the board.
- Use Clusters: Pair strong cheeses with strong accompaniments (e.g., blue cheese with walnuts and Port wine) in one section.
- Ventilation: If serving indoors, keep the area well-ventilated to disperse the aroma.

9. Avoiding Soggy Crackers and Bread

Crackers and bread can absorb moisture from nearby fruits, spreads, or cheeses.

Tips:

- Use Barriers: Place parchment paper or small bowls under moist items like fruits and spreads.
- Keep Bread Separate: Serve bread in a separate basket or tray.
- Layer Strategically: Arrange wet items away from crackers or bread to prevent sogginess.

10. Making a Stunning Presentation

A cheese board that looks unorganized may fail to impress, even if the flavors are perfect.

Tips:

- Create a Focal Point: Start with a centerpiece cheese or bowl of dip and build outward.

- Balance Colors: Distribute colorful fruits and garnishes evenly across the board.
- Layer and Stack: Use height and layers to create visual interest. For example, stack crackers or pile grapes for dimension.
- Use Garnishes: Add herbs, edible flowers, or decorative items to tie the look together.

11. Ensuring Enough for Everyone

It's easy to run out of popular items or end up with too much of something less popular.

Tips:

- Portion Planning: Plan for 1–2 ounces of cheese per person for appetizers, and 3–4 ounces for a main course.
- Replenish Strategically: Keep extra cheese and accompaniments ready to refill as items run low.
- Serve a Balanced Selection: Offer something for everyone—mild, bold, creamy, and hard cheeses.

12. Reducing Leftovers and Waste

Cheese boards often result in leftover items, especially if portions are too large.

Tips:

- Serve Smaller Portions: Start with smaller amounts and refill as needed.

- Plan for Versatility: Choose cheeses and accompaniments that can be repurposed in recipes (e.g., pasta, salads, or sandwiches).
- Encourage Guests to Take Home Leftovers: Provide small containers or bags for guests to take items they enjoyed.

13. Accommodating Dietary Restrictions

Guests with dietary needs might feel excluded if the board lacks suitable options.

Tips:

- Label Everything Clearly: Identify cheeses and accompaniments, noting gluten-free, vegan, or nut-free items.
- Separate Dietary Sections: Create a small, separate board for guests with specific restrictions.
- Offer Alternatives: Include vegan cheeses, gluten-free crackers, or nut-free snacks.

Tips for Storing Leftovers

Cheese boards are often overflowing with delicious items, and it's not uncommon to end up with leftovers. Properly storing leftover cheese and accompaniments ensures they stay fresh, flavorful, and ready for future enjoyment.

1. Storing Cheese

Cheese is delicate and needs the right conditions to maintain its flavor and texture. Here's how to store different types of cheese:

General Cheese Storage Tips:

- Use Cheese Paper or Parchment Paper: Avoid wrapping cheese in plastic wrap, as it traps moisture and can alter the flavor. Cheese paper or parchment paper allows the cheese to breathe while retaining its moisture.
- Avoid Direct Airflow: Store cheese in a sealed container or wrap it loosely with the paper and place it in a plastic or glass container to prevent it from drying out.
- Label and Date: Write the name of the cheese and the date it was stored to keep track of freshness.

By Cheese Type:

- Soft Cheeses (Brie, Camembert, Goat Cheese): Wrap in wax paper or parchment paper and store in an airtight container. Consume within 3–5 days.
- Semi-Soft Cheeses (Havarti, Gouda, Monterey Jack): Store wrapped in parchment or cheese paper, inside an airtight container. Consume within 7–10 days.
- Hard Cheeses (Cheddar, Parmesan, Gruyère): Wrap in parchment paper and cover with aluminum foil or place in an airtight container. Hard cheeses can last up to 3–4 weeks in the fridge.
- Blue Cheeses: Wrap loosely in wax or parchment paper and store in an airtight container to avoid the smell transferring to other foods. Consume within 7–10 days.

Freezing Cheese:

- Best for Hard Cheeses: Cheddar, Parmesan, and Gouda freeze well. Grate or cube the cheese before freezing and store it in a freezer-safe bag for up to 3 months.
- Avoid Freezing Soft Cheeses: Freezing changes the texture of Brie, Camembert, or goat cheese, making them less enjoyable for serving but still suitable for cooking.

2. Storing Crackers and Bread

Crackers and bread can become stale quickly if not stored properly.

- Crackers: Store in an airtight container or resealable plastic bag to keep them crispy. Place a silica gel packet (food-safe) in the container to absorb moisture if you live in a humid climate.
- Bread: Wrap leftover bread tightly in plastic wrap or aluminum foil and store at room temperature for 1–2 days. For longer storage, freeze the bread in a sealed bag for up to 3 months. Reheat in the oven for a fresh taste.

3. Storing Fruits and Vegetables

Fresh fruits and vegetables are best stored separately to maintain their texture and flavor.

Fresh Fruits:

- Grapes, berries, and apple slices: Store in a sealed container in the fridge and consume within 2–3 days.
- Prevent Browning: Toss apple or pear slices in lemon juice before storing to prevent browning.

- Dried Fruits: Place in an airtight container or resealable bag at room temperature. Dried fruits can last for weeks.

Vegetables:

- Cut vegetables (carrots, cucumbers, bell peppers): Store in a container with a damp paper towel to keep them crisp. Use within 3–5 days.

4. Storing Nuts

Store leftover nuts in an airtight container at room temperature for up to 2 weeks. For longer storage, refrigerate or freeze them to prevent them from going rancid. Nuts can be stored in the freezer for up to 6 months.

5. Storing Spreads and Condiments

Spreads and condiments like jams, honey, and chutneys often come in jars, making storage easy.

- Jams and Chutneys: Refrigerate in their original jars. Most can last for several weeks to months after opening.
- Honey: Store at room temperature in its original container. Honey doesn't spoil, but it may crystallize; gently warm the jar in hot water to liquefy it.
- Mustards and Dips: Refrigerate in airtight containers and consume within 1–2 weeks.

6. Storing Meats (If Used)

If your cheese board includes charcuterie, it's important to handle the leftovers properly.

- Cured Meats (Salami, Prosciutto, Chorizo): Wrap tightly in plastic wrap or place in an airtight container and refrigerate. Consume within 3–5 days.
- Cooked Meats (Bacon, Sausage): Store in airtight containers in the fridge and consume within 2–3 days.

7. Storing Garnishes and Decorative Items

- Herbs (Rosemary, Thyme, Basil): Wrap fresh herbs in a damp paper towel, place in a plastic bag, and refrigerate. Use within a few days.
- Edible Flowers: Store in an airtight container lined with damp paper towels in the fridge. Consume within 1–2 days.

8. Using Leftovers Creatively

Leftovers from your cheese board can be repurposed into delicious meals:

- Cheese: Use in omelets, sandwiches, pasta dishes, or salads.
- Crackers and Bread: Turn into breadcrumbs, croutons, or pair with soups.
- Fruits and Nuts: Add to yogurt, oatmeal, or baked goods.
- Spreads: Use as glazes for meats, or mix into sauces or desserts.

9. General Storage Tips

- Temperature: Always store perishable items like cheese and meats in the refrigerator at 35–45°F (1–7°C).
- Organize Properly: Place leftover cheese in the crisper drawer for optimal humidity levels.
- Don't Overstore: Leftovers are best enjoyed within a few days for peak freshness.

*** Recipe ***

Floral Spring Cheese Board

This cheese board brings the brightness of spring blooms with floral-infused cheeses, edible flowers, and fresh, vibrant accompaniments. Perfect for garden parties or a refreshing picnic.

Ingredients:

- 1 wheel of brie, topped with edible flowers
- 4 oz of lavender-infused goat cheese
- 4 oz of herb-coated cream cheese
- 1 cup of fresh strawberries and raspberries
- ½ cup of dried apricots
- ½ cup of candied walnuts
- Assorted crackers and a baguette, sliced
- Edible flowers for garnish

Directions:

1. Arrange the brie in the center of your cheese board and decorate it with edible flowers.
2. Slice the lavender-infused goat cheese and place it near the brie.
3. Add the herb-coated cream cheese in a small dish or as a spreadable option.
4. Surround the cheeses with fresh strawberries, raspberries, dried apricots, and candied walnuts.
5. Fill in gaps with crackers and baguette slices. Garnish with edible flowers for a spring touch.

Beverage Pairings:
Pair this board with a floral rosé, a sparkling elderflower cocktail, or chamomile tea.

Fresh Herb Cheese Board

Celebrate spring's herbs with this vibrant board, featuring cheeses and accompaniments infused with basil, thyme, and rosemary.

Ingredients:

- 4 oz of herbed chèvre (goat cheese)
- 6 oz of havarti with dill
- 4 oz of aged parmesan chunks
- 1 cup of fresh green grapes
- ½ cup of marinated olives
- ½ cup of roasted almonds
- 1 sprig of fresh rosemary for garnish
- Sliced sourdough bread

Directions:

1. Place the herbed chèvre in a small bowl or dish.
2. Arrange the havarti and parmesan in slices or chunks on the board.
3. Surround the cheeses with green grapes, marinated olives, and roasted almonds.
4. Add the sliced sourdough bread to the side. Garnish with a sprig of rosemary.

Beverage Pairings:
A crisp Sauvignon Blanc, a basil lemonade, or a light lager complements this cheese board beautifully.

Citrus Delight Cheese Board

This vibrant board combines citrus flavors with creamy cheeses, making it a refreshing option for spring gatherings.

Ingredients:

- 4 oz of lemon-infused ricotta cheese
- 6 oz of manchego
- 4 oz of orange-zest cheddar
- 1 cup of fresh orange and grapefruit slices
- ½ cup of dried mango
- ½ cup of honey-roasted cashews
- Assorted crackers and breadsticks

Directions:

1. Place the lemon-infused ricotta in a small dish and drizzle with honey.
2. Slice the manchego and orange-zest cheddar and arrange on the board.
3. Add the fresh orange and grapefruit slices for a pop of color.
4. Sprinkle the dried mango and honey-roasted cashews around the cheeses.
5. Add crackers and breadsticks to complete the board.

Beverage Pairings:
Pair with a citrus-forward white wine like Pinot Grigio, a mimosa, or sparkling water with a splash of orange juice.

Garden Veggie Cheese Board

This cheese board highlights the best of spring vegetables paired with creamy cheeses and tangy dips.

Ingredients:

- 4 oz of whipped feta
- 6 oz of soft brie
- 4 oz of aged cheddar
- 1 cup of fresh snap peas and radishes
- 1 cup of baby carrots and cherry tomatoes
- ½ cup of hummus
- ½ cup of pesto
- Sliced baguette and whole-grain crackers

Directions:

1. Place the whipped feta and hummus in small bowls on the board.
2. Arrange the brie and aged cheddar in slices or chunks.
3. Add snap peas, radishes, baby carrots, and cherry tomatoes around the cheeses and dips.
4. Place sliced baguette and crackers alongside the veggies. Garnish with fresh herbs like parsley or dill.

Beverage Pairings:
A crisp dry rosé, cucumber-infused water, or a light IPA pairs well with this board.

Sweet and Savory Spring Cheese Board

This cheese board offers a balance of sweet and savory flavors with a focus on seasonal produce and creamy cheeses.

Ingredients:

- 4 oz of camembert
- 6 oz of gouda
- 4 oz of honey-drizzled blue cheese
- 1 cup of fresh blackberries and figs
- ½ cup of apricot preserves
- ½ cup of pistachios
- 1 small loaf of artisan bread, sliced

Directions:

1. Arrange the camembert and gouda in the center of the board.
2. Slice the honey-drizzled blue cheese and place it nearby.
3. Add fresh blackberries, figs, and a small bowl of apricot preserves.
4. Sprinkle pistachios around the board and arrange artisan bread slices alongside the cheeses.

Beverage Pairings:
A sweet Moscato, a honey mead, or a sparkling lemonade pairs perfectly with this board.

Tropical Summer Cheese Board

This vibrant cheese board is a celebration of summer, featuring tropical fruits, creamy cheeses, and refreshing accompaniments. It's the perfect centerpiece for a warm evening gathering or a sunny afternoon by the pool.

Ingredients:

- 4 oz of creamy burrata
- 6 oz of aged white cheddar
- 4 oz of coconut gouda
- 1 cup of fresh mango slices
- 1 cup of pineapple chunks
- ½ cup of dried banana chips
- ½ cup of macadamia nuts
- ¼ cup of lime-infused honey for drizzling
- Assorted crackers and toasted coconut chips

Directions:

1. Place the burrata in a small dish on the cheese board and drizzle it with lime-infused honey.
2. Slice the aged white cheddar and coconut gouda into bite-sized pieces and arrange them on the board.
3. Add fresh mango slices and pineapple chunks for a tropical touch.
4. Sprinkle dried banana chips, macadamia nuts, and toasted coconut chips around the board to fill in the spaces.
5. Arrange crackers on the side for pairing with the cheeses.

Beverage Pairings:
Pair this summer board with a tropical white wine like Riesling, a piña colada, or a refreshing coconut water spritzer.

Cozy Winter Cheese Board

This winter-themed cheese board is rich and hearty, perfect for chilly evenings. It features bold flavors, seasonal fruits, and warm accompaniments to evoke the comfort of the season.

Ingredients:

- 6 oz of aged gouda
- 4 oz of blue cheese
- 6 oz of smoked cheddar
- 1 cup of fresh pear slices
- ½ cup of dried cranberries
- ½ cup of candied pecans
- ½ cup of fig jam
- 1 small loaf of crusty sourdough bread, sliced
- 1 sprig of fresh rosemary for garnish

Directions:

1. Arrange the aged gouda, blue cheese, and smoked cheddar on the cheese board, spacing them evenly.
2. Add the fresh pear slices and sprinkle dried cranberries around the cheeses.
3. Place candied pecans and a small dish of fig jam on the board.
4. Add slices of sourdough bread around the edges or in a separate basket.
5. Garnish the board with a sprig of fresh rosemary for a wintery touch.

Beverage Pairings:
Pair this board with a bold red wine like Cabernet Sauvignon, mulled wine, or a hot spiced cider for a cozy winter vibe.

Harvest Fall Cheese Board

This fall-themed cheese board celebrates the flavors of the season with warm, earthy tones, autumn fruits, and rustic accompaniments. It's perfect for gatherings around the fireplace or a Thanksgiving appetizer spread.

Ingredients:

- 4 oz of sharp aged cheddar
- 6 oz of creamy brie
- 4 oz of smoked gouda
- 1 cup of fresh apple slices (Honeycrisp or Fuji)
- 1 cup of fresh figs, halved
- ½ cup of dried apricots
- ½ cup of spiced candied pecans
- ¼ cup of pumpkin butter
- Assorted crackers and sliced baguette
- Fresh sage leaves for garnish

Directions:

1. Place the brie in the center of your cheese board and surround it with slices of sharp cheddar and smoked gouda.
2. Arrange the fresh apple slices, halved figs, and dried apricots around the cheeses.
3. Add the spiced candied pecans and a small dish of pumpkin butter to the board.
4. Fill in gaps with assorted crackers and baguette slices.
5. Garnish with fresh sage leaves to enhance the fall aesthetic.

Beverage Pairings:
Pair this board with a spiced cider, a warm mulled wine, or a light Pinot Noir for the perfect autumnal complement.

Elegant Sparkle Cheese Board

This board exudes elegance with sparkling touches, perfect for ringing in the New Year. Featuring a mix of luxurious cheeses and dazzling accompaniments, it's ideal for a midnight celebration.

Ingredients:

- 4 oz of triple cream brie
- 6 oz of aged parmesan chunks
- 4 oz of blue cheese
- ½ cup of candied almonds
- ½ cup of dried apricots
- 1 cup of fresh grapes (red and green mix)
- Edible gold leaf for garnish (optional)
- Assorted crackers

Directions:

1. Place the triple cream brie in the center and garnish with edible gold leaf for a sparkling touch.
2. Arrange the parmesan chunks and blue cheese slices around the brie.
3. Add the fresh grapes, dried apricots, and candied almonds around the cheeses.
4. Fill gaps with assorted crackers.

Beverage Pairings:
Pair with champagne, sparkling rosé, or a Prosecco cocktail.

Midnight Celebration Cheese Board

Bold and indulgent flavors take center stage on this cheese board, designed for sharing as the clock strikes midnight.

Ingredients:

- 4 oz of smoked gouda
- 6 oz of creamy camembert
- 4 oz of manchego
- 1 cup of fresh blackberries
- ½ cup of honey-roasted pistachios
- ½ cup of dark chocolate chunks
- ¼ cup of fig jam
- Sliced baguette and seeded crackers

Directions:

1. Place the camembert in a small dish and surround it with the smoked gouda and manchego slices.
2. Add blackberries, pistachios, and dark chocolate chunks around the cheeses.
3. Include a small bowl of fig jam for spreading, and arrange baguette slices and crackers around the board.

Beverage Pairings:
Pair with a bold red wine, sparkling sangria, or a dark chocolate stout.

Golden Hour Cheese Board

With golden hues and rich textures, this cheese board sets the tone for an opulent New Year's Eve.

Ingredients:

- 4 oz of sharp white cheddar
- 6 oz of gouda with truffle
- 4 oz of brie topped with honey and edible glitter
- ½ cup of dried pineapple
- ½ cup of candied pecans
- 1 cup of fresh pear slices
- Assorted crackers and breadsticks

Directions:

1. Place the brie in the center and drizzle with honey, topping it with edible glitter for a golden effect.
2. Arrange the sharp cheddar and truffle gouda slices around the brie.
3. Add fresh pear slices, dried pineapple, and candied pecans.
4. Fill gaps with crackers and breadsticks.

Beverage Pairings:
Pair with a sparkling white wine, a honey mead, or a golden ale.

Festive Countdown Cheese Board

This board is designed for sharing, featuring sweet and savory flavors to keep guests satisfied as they await the New Year.

Ingredients:

- 4 oz of herbed goat cheese
- 6 oz of aged gruyere
- 4 oz of cranberry-studded cheddar
- 1 cup of fresh apple slices
- ½ cup of dried cranberries
- ½ cup of spiced walnuts
- ¼ cup of red pepper jelly
- Assorted crackers and crostini

Directions:

1. Place the herbed goat cheese and cranberry cheddar in the center of the board.
2. Slice the aged gruyere and arrange it around the center.
3. Add apple slices, dried cranberries, and spiced walnuts around the cheeses.
4. Include a small dish of red pepper jelly and crackers to complete the board.

Beverage Pairings:
Pair with a festive cranberry punch, sparkling cider, or a light Pinot Noir.

Decadent New Year's Cheese Board

This luxurious cheese board features indulgent flavors to toast the New Year in style.

Ingredients:

- 4 oz of cambozola (a mix of brie and blue cheese)
- 6 oz of aged cheddar with caramelized onions
- 4 oz of nut-crusted goat cheese
- 1 cup of fresh pomegranate arils
- ½ cup of dark chocolate-covered almonds
- ½ cup of candied orange peels
- 1 small loaf of artisan bread, sliced
- Fresh thyme sprigs for garnish

Directions:

1. Arrange the cambozola, cheddar, and nut-crusted goat cheese on the board.
2. Add pomegranate arils, dark chocolate-covered almonds, and candied orange peels around the cheeses.
3. Place sliced artisan bread on one side of the board.
4. Garnish with fresh thyme sprigs for a festive touch.

Beverage Pairings:
Pair with a sweet Riesling, a classic martini, or a sparkling rosé.

Romantic Red Cheese Board

This cheese board is inspired by the colors of love, featuring vibrant reds and indulgent flavors for a romantic Valentine's Day evening.

Ingredients:

- 4 oz of cranberry-studded goat cheese
- 6 oz of aged gouda
- 4 oz of brie topped with raspberry preserves
- 1 cup of fresh strawberries and raspberries
- ½ cup of dried cherries
- ½ cup of dark chocolate truffles
- ¼ cup of rose petal-infused honey
- Assorted crackers

Directions:

1. Place the brie in the center of the board and top with raspberry preserves.
2. Slice the gouda and arrange it around the brie.
3. Add cranberry goat cheese to the side and surround it with fresh strawberries and raspberries.
4. Fill in gaps with dried cherries, dark chocolate truffles, and crackers.
5. Include a small dish of rose petal-infused honey for drizzling.

Beverage Pairings:
Pair with sparkling rosé, a berry-forward red wine, or a pomegranate spritzer.

Heartfelt Cheese Board

This board highlights heart-shaped elements, sweet and savory pairings, and a touch of elegance for Valentine's Day.

Ingredients:

- 6 oz of heart-shaped brie
- 4 oz of strawberry-flavored cream cheese
- 6 oz of aged cheddar
- 1 cup of fresh cherries, halved and pitted
- ½ cup of candied pecans
- ½ cup of dried strawberries
- ¼ cup of fig jam
- Sliced baguette and crackers

Directions:

1. Place the heart-shaped brie in the center of the board.
2. Spread the strawberry cream cheese in a small dish and place it nearby.
3. Slice the aged cheddar and arrange around the cheeses.
4. Add fresh cherries, dried strawberries, and candied pecans around the board.
5. Place crackers and baguette slices alongside the cheeses, and include a small bowl of fig jam.

Beverage Pairings:
Pair with a light Pinot Noir, strawberry champagne, or a hibiscus mocktail.

Sweet & Savory Love Board

This cheese board balances sweet and savory flavors, creating a perfect harmony for a Valentine's Day date night.

Ingredients:

- 4 oz of honey-drizzled goat cheese
- 6 oz of smoked gouda
- 4 oz of manchego
- 1 cup of fresh blackberries and raspberries
- ½ cup of dark chocolate-covered almonds
- ½ cup of marinated olives
- ¼ cup of chili honey for drizzling
- Whole-grain crackers

Directions:

1. Place the honey-drizzled goat cheese in the center of the board.
2. Slice the smoked gouda and manchego and arrange them around the goat cheese.
3. Add fresh blackberries, raspberries, and dark chocolate-covered almonds.
4. Place marinated olives in a small bowl and add crackers to the side.
5. Drizzle the chili honey over the goat cheese for a spicy-sweet touch.

Beverage Pairings:
Pair with a bold red wine, spiced mulled wine, or a blackberry-infused cocktail.

Blush Pink Cheese Board

Celebrate Valentine's Day with a board showcasing pink hues and creamy, luxurious textures that feel as indulgent as the occasion.

Ingredients:

- 4 oz of rosé-infused goat cheese
- 6 oz of camembert
- 4 oz of white cheddar
- 1 cup of fresh watermelon cubes
- ½ cup of pink champagne gummies
- ½ cup of pistachios
- ¼ cup of raspberry jam
- Water crackers and breadsticks

Directions:

1. Place the camembert in the center and surround it with the rosé-infused goat cheese and white cheddar slices.
2. Add watermelon cubes, pink champagne gummies, and pistachios around the cheeses.
3. Include a small bowl of raspberry jam for spreading and arrange water crackers and breadsticks along the edges.

Beverage Pairings:
Pair with sparkling rosé, a watermelon margarita, or pink lemonade.

Decadent Chocolate & Cheese Board

For couples who love chocolate, this board combines rich cheeses and decadent chocolate pairings for an indulgent Valentine's Day treat.

Ingredients:

- 4 oz of chocolate-rubbed cheese (such as BellaVitano)
- 6 oz of mascarpone cheese
- 4 oz of brie topped with dark chocolate shavings
- 1 cup of fresh strawberries and blueberries
- ½ cup of chocolate-covered pretzels
- ½ cup of hazelnuts
- ¼ cup of honey for drizzling
- Assorted cookies and crackers

Directions:

1. Place the chocolate-rubbed cheese in the center of the board.
2. Spread mascarpone cheese in a small dish for dipping or spreading.
3. Top the brie with dark chocolate shavings and place it near the center.
4. Add fresh strawberries, blueberries, chocolate-covered pretzels, and hazelnuts around the cheeses.
5. Arrange cookies and crackers along the edges and drizzle honey over the mascarpone for a sweet finish.

Beverage Pairings:

Pair with a chocolate martini, a sweet red dessert wine, or a hot chocolate with a splash of liqueur.

Spooky Charcuterie Cheese Board

This cheese board brings the Halloween spirit with creepy accents, dark colors, and seasonal flavors. Perfect for any haunted gathering!

Ingredients:

- 4 oz of aged gouda (cut into bat shapes using a cookie cutter)
- 6 oz of brie, topped with blackberry preserves for a "bloody" effect
- 4 oz of black garlic cheddar
- 1 cup of fresh blackberries and blueberries
- ½ cup of dried apricots
- ½ cup of spiced candied pecans
- Black sesame crackers and charcoal bread slices
- Plastic spider rings or Halloween-themed garnishes

Directions:

1. Place the brie in the center of the board and spread blackberry preserves on top to create a "bloody" effect.
2. Arrange bat-shaped gouda slices and black garlic cheddar around the brie.
3. Add blackberries, blueberries, dried apricots, and candied pecans around the board.
4. Fill gaps with black sesame crackers and charcoal bread slices.
5. Add plastic spiders or themed garnishes for a spooky touch.

Beverage Pairings:
Pair with a dark red wine like Malbec, a blackberry sangria, or a Halloween-themed cocktail like a Black Widow Martini.

Pumpkin Patch Cheese Board

This festive board celebrates Halloween with pumpkin-shaped cheeses and autumnal flavors for a cozy, spooky vibe.

Ingredients:

- 4 oz of pumpkin-shaped cheddar (use a pumpkin cookie cutter)
- 6 oz of herbed goat cheese, rolled into "mini pumpkins" and coated in paprika
- 4 oz of smoked gouda
- 1 cup of fresh apple slices
- ½ cup of dried cranberries
- ½ cup of roasted pumpkin seeds
- Mini pretzel sticks (for stems in goat cheese pumpkins)
- Sliced baguette and crackers

Directions:

1. Create mini pumpkins by rolling herbed goat cheese into small balls, coating them in paprika, and inserting mini pretzel sticks as stems.
2. Arrange pumpkin-shaped cheddar and smoked gouda slices on the board.
3. Surround the cheeses with apple slices, dried cranberries, and roasted pumpkin seeds.
4. Add sliced baguette and crackers to complete the board.

Beverage Pairings:
Pair with a pumpkin ale, spiced cider, or a bourbon-based fall cocktail.

Graveyard Cheese Board

This eerie cheese board features tombstone-shaped cheeses and dark, moody elements for a haunting presentation.

Ingredients:

- 4 oz of havarti, cut into tombstone shapes
- 6 oz of manchego
- 4 oz of ash-rubbed goat cheese (for a spooky, grayish effect)
- 1 cup of fresh purple grapes
- ½ cup of fig jam
- ½ cup of dark chocolate almonds
- Black crackers and breadsticks
- Edible rosemary sprigs for garnish

Directions:

1. Use a knife to shape havarti into tombstones and place them upright in the cheese board.
2. Arrange manchego slices and ash-rubbed goat cheese around the tombstones.
3. Add purple grapes, fig jam, and dark chocolate almonds.
4. Place black crackers and breadsticks around the edges and garnish with rosemary sprigs for a "graveyard" effect.

Beverage Pairings:
Pair with a bold Cabernet Sauvignon, a blackberry mojito, or a smoky mezcal cocktail.

Witch's Cauldron Cheese Board

This witchy cheese board incorporates bold flavors and eerie accents to delight your Halloween guests.

Ingredients:

- 4 oz of blue cheese (crumbled for a bubbling "cauldron" effect)
- 6 oz of sharp white cheddar
- 4 oz of truffle brie
- 1 cup of fresh figs, halved
- ½ cup of spiced nuts
- ½ cup of olives stuffed with red pimento (for "eyeballs")
- Crackers and breadsticks
- Small plastic cauldron (optional)

Directions:

1. Place the blue cheese in a small bowl or plastic cauldron to resemble bubbling potion.
2. Slice the white cheddar and truffle brie, and arrange them around the cauldron.
3. Add halved figs, spiced nuts, and olives around the board for spooky accents.
4. Arrange crackers and breadsticks to complete the board.

Beverage Pairings:
Pair with a witch's brew sangria, an herbal gin cocktail, or a dry Prosecco.

Monster Mash Cheese Board

This playful cheese board features monster-themed elements and vibrant colors, making it a hit with kids and adults alike.

Ingredients:

- 4 oz of Colby Jack, cut into monster face shapes with cookie cutters
- 6 oz of mozzarella balls ("eyeballs" with black olive slices)
- 4 oz of pepper jack cheese
- 1 cup of fresh carrot sticks and celery
- ½ cup of dried mango strips
- ½ cup of chocolate-covered pretzels
- Assorted crackers

Directions:

1. Cut Colby Jack into monster faces using Halloween cookie cutters or a knife.
2. Create "eyeballs" by topping mozzarella balls with black olive slices and arranging them on the board.
3. Slice the pepper jack and add it alongside the Colby Jack.
4. Surround the cheese with carrot sticks, celery, dried mango strips, and chocolate-covered pretzels.
5. Fill gaps with assorted crackers for a complete spread.

Beverage Pairings:
Pair with a fun green apple punch, a non-alcoholic sparkling cider, or a blood orange mocktail.

Holiday Wreath Cheese Board

This festive cheese board is shaped like a holiday wreath, featuring seasonal ingredients in red, green, and white for a beautiful centerpiece.

Ingredients:

- 4 oz of herbed goat cheese
- 6 oz of white cheddar, cubed
- 4 oz of brie, cut into wedges
- 1 cup of fresh cherry tomatoes and green grapes
- ½ cup of dried cranberries
- ½ cup of roasted pistachios
- Fresh rosemary sprigs for garnish
- Assorted crackers

Directions:

1. Arrange fresh rosemary sprigs in a circular shape on the board to form the wreath base.
2. Place goat cheese, cheddar cubes, and brie wedges around the wreath.
3. Add cherry tomatoes, green grapes, dried cranberries, and pistachios to fill in the gaps.
4. Scatter crackers along the edges for easy serving.

Beverage Pairings:
Pair with a crisp Sauvignon Blanc, a holiday spiced sangria, or a sparkling cranberry cocktail.

Snowy Christmas Cheese Board

This board evokes the beauty of a snowy winter with creamy white cheeses and frosty accompaniments.

Ingredients:

- 4 oz of camembert, topped with a drizzle of honey
- 6 oz of aged manchego
- 4 oz of white stilton with cranberries
- 1 cup of fresh pear slices
- ½ cup of sugared cranberries
- ½ cup of candied pecans
- Snowflake-shaped crackers or classic water crackers

Directions:

1. Place camembert in the center and drizzle with honey for a frosty effect.
2. Arrange manchego and stilton slices around the camembert.
3. Add fresh pear slices, sugared cranberries, and candied pecans to the board.
4. Fill gaps with snowflake-shaped crackers.

Beverage Pairings:
Pair with a sparkling white wine, a pear cider, or an eggnog cocktail.

Christmas Tree Cheese Board

This cheese board is arranged in the shape of a Christmas tree, featuring vibrant layers of cheeses, fruits, and nuts for a festive holiday spread.

Ingredients:

- 4 oz of sharp cheddar, cubed
- 6 oz of gouda, sliced
- 4 oz of havarti with dill
- 1 cup of green grapes
- ½ cup of dried apricots
- ½ cup of roasted almonds
- 1 small star-shaped cookie cutter
- Breadsticks for the tree trunk

Directions:

1. Use the star-shaped cookie cutter to cut a star out of a slice of cheddar and place it at the top of the board.
2. Arrange layers of cheddar cubes, gouda slices, havarti, grapes, and dried apricots in a triangular "tree" shape.
3. Sprinkle roasted almonds throughout the tree.
4. Use breadsticks at the bottom to create the tree trunk.

Beverage Pairings:
Pair with a mulled wine, a light Chardonnay, or a cinnamon-spiced mocktail.

Candy Cane Cheese Board

This playful cheese board mimics the stripes of a candy cane using alternating slices of cheese and cured meats.

Ingredients:

- 6 oz of mozzarella slices
- 6 oz of sharp cheddar slices
- 6 oz of prosciutto or salami slices
- ½ cup of dried cranberries
- ½ cup of pistachios
- Assorted crackers

Directions:

1. Arrange mozzarella slices and prosciutto in an alternating pattern to form the shape of a candy cane.
2. Place cheddar slices alongside the candy cane for additional flavor options.
3. Add dried cranberries and pistachios as accents around the candy cane.
4. Include crackers on the side for easy pairing.

Beverage Pairings:
Pair with a cranberry mimosa, a sparkling rosé, or a festive holiday punch.

Warm & Cozy Christmas Cheese Board

This cheese board is full of rich, comforting flavors and pairs perfectly with the cozy ambiance of the holiday season.

Ingredients:

- 4 oz of smoked gouda
- 6 oz of aged cheddar with caramelized onions
- 4 oz of brie, baked and topped with cranberry sauce
- 1 cup of fresh apple slices
- ½ cup of roasted pecans
- ½ cup of dark chocolate chunks
- Sliced baguette and seeded crackers

Directions:

1. Bake the brie in the oven at 350°F (175°C) for 10 minutes, then top it with cranberry sauce. Place it in the center of the board.
2. Arrange smoked gouda and caramelized onion cheddar slices around the brie.
3. Add fresh apple slices, roasted pecans, and dark chocolate chunks around the cheeses.
4. Include sliced baguette and crackers on the side for pairing.

Beverage Pairings:
Pair with a classic red blend, hot mulled wine, or a spiced cider.

Harvest Feast Cheese Board

This board highlights the flavors of Thanksgiving with a blend of seasonal fruits, nuts, and rich, comforting cheeses. It's perfect as an appetizer before the big feast.

Ingredients:

- 4 oz of sharp white cheddar
- 6 oz of gouda with truffle
- 4 oz of brie topped with a drizzle of honey
- 1 cup of fresh apple and pear slices
- ½ cup of dried cranberries
- ½ cup of spiced candied pecans
- Sliced baguette and whole-grain crackers

Directions:

1. Place the brie in the center of the board and drizzle with honey.
2. Arrange the cheddar and gouda slices around the brie.
3. Add fresh apple and pear slices, dried cranberries, and spiced candied pecans.
4. Fill gaps with baguette slices and crackers.

Beverage Pairings:
Pair with a crisp apple cider, a light Pinot Noir, or a dry Riesling.

Turkey Day Cheese Board

This Thanksgiving-themed board features festive shapes and warm autumnal flavors, perfect for a pre-dinner snack.

Ingredients:

- 6 oz of havarti, cut into turkey shapes using a cookie cutter
- 4 oz of cranberry goat cheese log
- 6 oz of aged manchego
- 1 cup of fresh red grapes
- ½ cup of roasted pumpkin seeds
- ½ cup of fig jam
- Assorted crackers and breadsticks

Directions:

1. Use a cookie cutter to cut havarti into turkey shapes and arrange them on the board.
2. Slice the cranberry goat cheese and manchego and place them around the turkey shapes.
3. Add red grapes, pumpkin seeds, and fig jam in small clusters around the cheeses.
4. Fill in the gaps with crackers and breadsticks.

Beverage Pairings:
Pair with a dry rosé, a spiced pumpkin ale, or a pear spritzer.

Cornucopia Cheese Board

Designed to look like a traditional cornucopia, this board overflows with the bounty of the season, showcasing cheeses, fruits, and nuts.

Ingredients:

- 4 oz of smoked gouda
- 6 oz of sharp cheddar cubes
- 4 oz of creamy blue cheese
- 1 cup of fresh figs and pomegranate arils
- ½ cup of dried apricots
- ½ cup of candied walnuts
- Sliced multigrain bread and crackers
- Edible rosemary sprigs for garnish

Directions:

1. Arrange cheeses in a fan shape to mimic the opening of a cornucopia.
2. Place figs, pomegranate arils, dried apricots, and candied walnuts around the cheeses in an overflowing pattern.
3. Add bread slices and crackers on one side of the board.
4. Garnish with rosemary sprigs for a festive touch.

Beverage Pairings:
Pair with a bold Cabernet Sauvignon, a spiced cranberry cocktail, or hot mulled wine.

Thankful Gathering Cheese Board

This board brings together comforting cheeses and rich, hearty flavors, perfect for celebrating gratitude with loved ones.

Ingredients:

- 4 oz of smoked cheddar
- 6 oz of brie topped with cranberry chutney
- 4 oz of aged gouda
- 1 cup of fresh green apple slices
- ½ cup of dried cherries
- ½ cup of caramelized pecans
- Assorted crackers and breadsticks

Directions:

1. Place the brie in the center of the board and top it with cranberry chutney.
2. Arrange smoked cheddar slices and aged gouda chunks around the brie.
3. Add green apple slices, dried cherries, and caramelized pecans to the board.
4. Fill in gaps with crackers and breadsticks.

Beverage Pairings:
Pair with a light Chardonnay, a hard apple cider, or a bourbon-spiked punch.

Autumn Colors Cheese Board

This board is inspired by the vibrant colors of fall, combining rich cheeses with bright fruits and nuts to bring Thanksgiving to life.

Ingredients:

- 4 oz of cranberry-studded white stilton
- 6 oz of aged gruyere
- 4 oz of camembert
- 1 cup of fresh persimmon slices and red grapes
- ½ cup of dried mango strips
- ½ cup of pistachios
- Sliced rye bread and crackers

Directions:

1. Place the camembert in the center and surround it with slices of aged gruyere and cranberry-studded white stilton.
2. Add persimmon slices, red grapes, and dried mango strips around the cheeses.
3. Sprinkle pistachios throughout the board.
4. Include sliced rye bread and crackers along the edges.

Beverage Pairings:
Pair with a sparkling white wine, a cranberry mojito, or a festive fall sangria.

Classic Keto Cheese Board

This cheese board is perfect for those on a keto diet, offering a mix of low-carb cheeses, nuts, and keto-friendly accompaniments for any occasion.

Ingredients:

- 4 oz of sharp cheddar
- 6 oz of brie
- 4 oz of gouda
- ½ cup of marinated olives
- ½ cup of roasted almonds
- 1 cup of sliced cucumber and radishes
- ¼ cup of keto-friendly mustard or aioli

Directions:

1. Arrange the cheddar, brie, and gouda on the cheese board in separate sections.
2. Add the marinated olives and roasted almonds around the cheeses.
3. Place cucumber slices and radishes for freshness.
4. Include a small bowl of keto-friendly mustard or aioli for dipping.

Beverage Pairings:
Pair with a dry white wine, sparkling water with lime, or a sugar-free gin cocktail.

Mediterranean Keto Cheese Board

This keto cheese board has Mediterranean flavors, featuring rich cheeses, olives, and fresh vegetables for a light and satisfying snack.

Ingredients:

- 4 oz of feta cheese
- 6 oz of manchego
- 4 oz of halloumi, grilled and sliced
- ½ cup of marinated artichoke hearts
- ½ cup of green and black olives
- 1 cup of sliced bell peppers and zucchini
- Fresh rosemary sprigs for garnish

Directions:

1. Arrange feta and manchego on the board and place grilled halloumi slices nearby.
2. Add marinated artichoke hearts and a mix of green and black olives around the cheeses.
3. Include sliced bell peppers and zucchini for a pop of color and crunch.
4. Garnish with fresh rosemary sprigs for a Mediterranean touch.

Beverage Pairings:
Pair with a dry rosé, a sparkling mineral water, or a keto mojito.

Spicy Keto Cheese Board

This cheese board combines bold, spicy flavors with creamy cheeses and crunchy keto-friendly snacks for a fiery twist.

Ingredients:

- 4 oz of pepper jack cheese
- 6 oz of aged cheddar with chili flakes
- 4 oz of spicy herbed goat cheese
- ½ cup of roasted spicy pecans
- ½ cup of marinated jalapeños
- 1 cup of sliced celery and jicama sticks
- ¼ cup of sugar-free hot sauce or salsa for dipping

Directions:

1. Place pepper jack, cheddar, and herbed goat cheese on the board.
2. Add roasted spicy pecans and marinated jalapeños for a fiery touch.
3. Arrange celery and jicama sticks around the cheeses.
4. Include a small dish of sugar-free hot sauce or salsa for dipping.

Beverage Pairings:
Pair with a keto margarita, a dry red wine, or sparkling water with jalapeño slices.

Keto Charcuterie Cheese Board

This cheese board pairs keto-friendly cheeses with a variety of meats, nuts, and pickles for a hearty and satisfying snack.

Ingredients:

- 4 oz of aged parmesan
- 6 oz of smoked gouda
- 4 oz of camembert
- 6 slices of prosciutto
- 6 slices of salami
- ½ cup of cornichons (small pickles)
- ½ cup of roasted macadamia nuts
- Fresh arugula leaves for garnish

Directions:

1. Arrange parmesan, smoked gouda, and camembert on the board.
2. Fold prosciutto and salami slices and place them around the cheeses.
3. Add cornichons and roasted macadamia nuts to fill in gaps.
4. Garnish with fresh arugula leaves for color and freshness.

Beverage Pairings:
Pair with a dry Prosecco, a keto-friendly Old Fashioned, or lemon-infused sparkling water.

Keto Sweet & Savory Cheese Board

This board offers a balance of sweet and savory keto-friendly flavors, perfect for those craving variety while staying low-carb.

Ingredients:

- 4 oz of blue cheese
- 6 oz of creamy brie
- 4 oz of goat cheese with herbs
- ½ cup of blackberries and raspberries (low-carb fruits)
- ½ cup of keto chocolate chunks
- ½ cup of roasted walnuts
- ¼ cup of sugar-free raspberry jam
- Low-carb crackers or cheese crisps

Directions:

1. Place the blue cheese, brie, and goat cheese on the board.
2. Add blackberries, raspberries, and roasted walnuts around the cheeses.
3. Place keto chocolate chunks and a small dish of sugar-free raspberry jam nearby.
4. Include low-carb crackers or cheese crisps for crunch.

Beverage Pairings:
Pair with a keto-friendly red wine, sparkling water with berries, or a sugar-free chocolate martini.

Festive Vegan Cheese Board

This vibrant vegan cheese board is perfect for celebrations, featuring a mix of plant-based cheeses, fresh fruits, and crunchy accompaniments.

Ingredients:

- 4 oz of cashew-based brie
- 6 oz of almond-based cheddar
- 4 oz of herb-crusted vegan cream cheese
- 1 cup of fresh grapes and blackberries
- ½ cup of dried apricots
- ½ cup of spiced candied pecans
- Gluten-free crackers and sliced baguette

Directions:

1. Arrange the cashew-based brie in the center of the board.
2. Slice the almond-based cheddar and place it around the brie.
3. Add dollops of herb-crusted vegan cream cheese in small clusters.
4. Surround the cheeses with fresh grapes, blackberries, dried apricots, and candied pecans.
5. Fill gaps with crackers and baguette slices.

Beverage Pairings:
Pair with a crisp Sauvignon Blanc, sparkling water with lime, or a light kombucha.

Mediterranean Vegan Cheese Board

Inspired by Mediterranean flavors, this vegan cheese board combines creamy dairy-free cheeses with marinated vegetables and olives.

Ingredients:

- 4 oz of cashew-based feta
- 6 oz of coconut-based mozzarella, sliced
- 4 oz of vegan smoked gouda
- ½ cup of marinated artichoke hearts
- ½ cup of green and black olives
- 1 cup of cherry tomatoes and cucumber slices
- Fresh rosemary sprigs for garnish

Directions:

1. Place the cashew-based feta in a small dish.
2. Arrange the sliced coconut mozzarella and smoked gouda around the feta.
3. Add marinated artichoke hearts, olives, and cherry tomatoes.
4. Fill in gaps with cucumber slices and garnish with fresh rosemary sprigs.

Beverage Pairings:
Pair with a dry rosé, sparkling mineral water, or a lemon and mint iced tea.

Spicy Vegan Cheese Board

This board offers bold, spicy flavors and creamy vegan cheeses, making it a hit for spice lovers.

Ingredients:

- 4 oz of chili-infused vegan cream cheese
- 6 oz of jalapeño-flavored vegan cheddar
- 4 oz of smoky cashew cheese spread
- ½ cup of roasted spicy pecans
- ½ cup of marinated jalapeños
- 1 cup of celery and carrot sticks
- Gluten-free crackers

Directions:

1. Place the chili-infused vegan cream cheese in a small bowl in the center of the board.
2. Slice the jalapeño-flavored cheddar and arrange it around the bowl.
3. Add the smoky cashew cheese spread in dollops or in a small dish.
4. Surround the cheeses with spicy pecans, marinated jalapeños, and celery and carrot sticks.
5. Add gluten-free crackers for crunch.

Beverage Pairings:
Pair with a sugar-free margarita, a smoky mezcal cocktail, or sparkling water with jalapeño slices.

Sweet & Savory Vegan Cheese Board

This vegan cheese board is a delightful mix of sweet and savory flavors, making it perfect for a balanced snack or dessert.

Ingredients:

- 4 oz of cashew-based blue cheese
- 6 oz of coconut-based cream cheese topped with a drizzle of maple syrup
- 4 oz of vegan white cheddar
- 1 cup of fresh figs and raspberries
- ½ cup of dark chocolate chunks
- ½ cup of roasted almonds
- Gluten-free breadsticks and crackers

Directions:

1. Place the coconut-based cream cheese in the center of the board and drizzle it with maple syrup.
2. Arrange the cashew-based blue cheese and vegan white cheddar around it.
3. Add fresh figs, raspberries, dark chocolate chunks, and roasted almonds around the cheeses.
4. Include breadsticks and crackers on the edges for variety.

Beverage Pairings:
Pair with a vegan dessert wine, sparkling water with berries, or a cinnamon-spiced chai tea.

Holiday Vegan Cheese Board

This festive vegan cheese board combines holiday-inspired flavors, seasonal fruits, and nut-based cheeses for a cozy and indulgent treat.

Ingredients:

- 4 oz of cashew-based brie topped with cranberry sauce
- 6 oz of almond-based gouda
- 4 oz of herb-crusted cashew cheese
- 1 cup of sliced apples and pears
- ½ cup of sugared cranberries
- ½ cup of candied walnuts
- Gluten-free crackers

Directions:

1. Place the cashew-based brie in the center and top it with cranberry sauce.
2. Slice the almond-based gouda and arrange it around the brie.
3. Add dollops of herb-crusted cashew cheese in small clusters.
4. Surround the cheeses with sliced apples, pears, sugared cranberries, and candied walnuts.
5. Fill gaps with gluten-free crackers.

Beverage Pairings:
Pair with a vegan-friendly sparkling wine, hot mulled cider, or a cranberry spritzer.

Classic Gluten-Free Cheese Board

This simple and elegant cheese board features gluten-free ingredients and a variety of textures and flavors, perfect for entertaining.

Ingredients:

- 4 oz of sharp white cheddar
- 6 oz of brie
- 4 oz of gouda
- 1 cup of fresh grapes and apple slices
- ½ cup of dried apricots
- ½ cup of roasted almonds
- Gluten-free crackers

Directions:

1. Arrange the cheddar, brie, and gouda in separate sections of the board.
2. Add fresh grapes, apple slices, dried apricots, and roasted almonds around the cheeses.
3. Fill in gaps with gluten-free crackers for pairing.

Beverage Pairings:
Pair with a crisp Sauvignon Blanc, sparkling water with citrus, or a light cider.

Mediterranean Gluten-Free Cheese Board

This gluten-free cheese board brings Mediterranean-inspired flavors with marinated vegetables, olives, and creamy cheeses.

Ingredients:

- 4 oz of feta cheese (crumbled or block)
- 6 oz of manchego
- 4 oz of herbed goat cheese
- ½ cup of marinated artichoke hearts
- ½ cup of olives (green and black mix)
- 1 cup of cucumber and bell pepper slices
- Gluten-free flatbread crackers

Directions:

1. Arrange the feta, manchego, and herbed goat cheese on the board.
2. Add marinated artichoke hearts and olives around the cheeses.
3. Fill in with cucumber and bell pepper slices for freshness and color.
4. Include gluten-free flatbread crackers for a Mediterranean pairing.

Beverage Pairings:
Pair with a dry rosé, sparkling mineral water, or a lemon and mint iced tea.

Autumn Harvest Gluten-Free Cheese Board

This seasonal board features comforting fall flavors and gluten-free ingredients for a cozy and delicious spread.

Ingredients:

- 4 oz of smoked gouda
- 6 oz of aged cheddar
- 4 oz of brie topped with fig jam
- 1 cup of fresh apple and pear slices
- ½ cup of spiced candied pecans
- ½ cup of dried cranberries
- Gluten-free seed crackers

Directions:

1. Place the brie in the center of the board and top with fig jam.
2. Arrange smoked gouda and aged cheddar slices around the brie.
3. Add apple slices, pear slices, dried cranberries, and spiced candied pecans around the cheeses.
4. Fill in gaps with gluten-free seed crackers.

Beverage Pairings:
Pair with a bold red wine, hot mulled cider, or a spiced pumpkin ale.

Spicy Gluten-Free Cheese Board

This cheese board offers a kick of spice with bold cheeses and zesty accompaniments, all gluten-free for an indulgent treat.

Ingredients:

- 4 oz of pepper jack cheese
- 6 oz of sharp cheddar with chili flakes
- 4 oz of smoky gouda
- ½ cup of marinated jalapeños
- ½ cup of roasted spicy pecans
- 1 cup of celery and carrot sticks
- Gluten-free tortilla chips

Directions:

1. Arrange the pepper jack, cheddar, and gouda on the board.
2. Add marinated jalapeños and roasted spicy pecans around the cheeses.
3. Place celery and carrot sticks for a fresh crunch.
4. Include gluten-free tortilla chips for dipping or pairing.

Beverage Pairings:
Pair with a margarita mocktail, a spicy red blend, or sparkling water with lime.

Sweet & Savory Gluten-Free Cheese Board

This cheese board combines sweet and savory gluten-free options for a well-balanced and satisfying spread.

Ingredients:

- 4 oz of blue cheese
- 6 oz of creamy goat cheese topped with honey
- 4 oz of sharp white cheddar
- 1 cup of fresh strawberries and blackberries
- ½ cup of dark chocolate chunks
- ½ cup of roasted walnuts
- Gluten-free crackers

Directions:

1. Place the goat cheese in the center of the board and drizzle with honey.
2. Arrange blue cheese and sharp cheddar slices around the goat cheese.
3. Add fresh strawberries, blackberries, dark chocolate chunks, and roasted walnuts around the cheeses.
4. Fill in gaps with gluten-free crackers for pairing.

Beverage Pairings:
Pair with a sweet Riesling, sparkling water with berries, or a hot cinnamon tea.

Classic Low-Lactose Cheese Board

This cheese board features a selection of low-lactose cheeses and light accompaniments, perfect for those sensitive to dairy but still craving a classic spread.

Ingredients:

- 4 oz of aged cheddar (low-lactose)
- 6 oz of Parmesan chunks (naturally low-lactose)
- 4 oz of manchego (aged)
- 1 cup of fresh grapes and apple slices
- ½ cup of roasted almonds
- ½ cup of dried apricots
- Gluten-free crackers or breadsticks

Directions:

1. Arrange the cheddar, Parmesan, and manchego on the board in separate sections.
2. Add grapes, apple slices, roasted almonds, and dried apricots around the cheeses.
3. Fill gaps with crackers or breadsticks.

Beverage Pairings:
Pair with a crisp Sauvignon Blanc, sparkling water with lemon, or a light cider.

Mediterranean Low-Lactose Cheese Board

Inspired by Mediterranean flavors, this cheese board combines lactose-friendly cheeses with fresh, light accompaniments.

Ingredients:

- 4 oz of aged goat cheese
- 6 oz of manchego
- 4 oz of lactose-free feta
- ½ cup of marinated olives
- ½ cup of roasted red peppers
- 1 cup of cucumber and cherry tomato slices
- Gluten-free seed crackers

Directions:

1. Place the goat cheese, manchego, and feta in separate sections of the board.
2. Add marinated olives and roasted red peppers around the cheeses.
3. Arrange cucumber and cherry tomato slices for color and freshness.
4. Include seed crackers for pairing.

Beverage Pairings:
Pair with a dry rosé, sparkling water with mint, or a Mediterranean-inspired white wine.

Sweet & Savory Low-Lactose Cheese Board

This cheese board balances sweet and savory flavors with lactose-friendly cheeses and light accompaniments.

Ingredients:

- 4 oz of aged Swiss cheese
- 6 oz of Parmesan wedges
- 4 oz of lactose-free cream cheese topped with honey
- 1 cup of fresh strawberries and figs
- ½ cup of candied walnuts
- ½ cup of dark chocolate chunks (dairy-free)
- Gluten-free crackers

Directions:

1. Place the lactose-free cream cheese in a small dish and drizzle with honey.
2. Arrange the Swiss cheese and Parmesan wedges around the cream cheese.
3. Add strawberries, figs, candied walnuts, and dark chocolate chunks around the cheeses.
4. Fill in gaps with crackers.

Beverage Pairings:
Pair with a sweet Riesling, sparkling rosé, or a berry-infused mocktail.

Low-Lactose Spicy Cheese Board

This board is ideal for those who love a bit of spice, featuring low-lactose cheeses with bold, fiery flavors.

Ingredients:

- 4 oz of lactose-free pepper jack cheese
- 6 oz of aged cheddar with chili flakes
- 4 oz of smoked gouda (low-lactose)
- ½ cup of marinated jalapeños
- ½ cup of spiced pecans
- 1 cup of celery and carrot sticks
- Gluten-free tortilla chips

Directions:

1. Arrange the pepper jack, aged cheddar, and smoked gouda on the board.
2. Add marinated jalapeños and spiced pecans around the cheeses.
3. Place celery and carrot sticks for freshness.
4. Include gluten-free tortilla chips for crunch.

Beverage Pairings:
Pair with a spicy margarita mocktail, a bold red wine, or sparkling water with lime.

Low-Lactose Holiday Cheese Board

This festive cheese board combines holiday-inspired flavors with lactose-friendly cheeses and seasonal accompaniments.

Ingredients:

- 4 oz of aged cheddar
- 6 oz of lactose-free Swiss cheese
- 4 oz of lactose-free brie topped with cranberry sauce
- 1 cup of fresh apple and pear slices
- ½ cup of sugared cranberries
- ½ cup of roasted pecans
- Gluten-free crackers

Directions:

1. Place the lactose-free brie in the center of the board and top it with cranberry sauce.
2. Arrange the cheddar and Swiss cheese slices around the brie.
3. Add apple slices, pear slices, sugared cranberries, and roasted pecans around the cheeses.
4. Fill in gaps with gluten-free crackers.

Beverage Pairings:
Pair with a sparkling white wine, hot cider, or a festive cranberry spritzer.

Classic Nut-Free Cheese Board

This simple cheese board offers a variety of cheeses and nut-free accompaniments for a universally enjoyable spread, perfect for any gathering.

Ingredients:

- 4 oz of aged cheddar
- 6 oz of creamy brie
- 4 oz of gouda
- 1 cup of fresh grapes and apple slices
- ½ cup of dried apricots
- ½ cup of sunflower seeds (nut-free alternative)
- Gluten-free crackers

Directions:

1. Arrange the cheddar, brie, and gouda on the board in separate sections.
2. Add fresh grapes, apple slices, dried apricots, and sunflower seeds around the cheeses.
3. Fill gaps with gluten-free crackers.

Beverage Pairings:
Pair with a crisp white wine like Sauvignon Blanc, sparkling water with lime, or a light apple cider.

Mediterranean Nut-Free Cheese Board

This Mediterranean-inspired nut-free cheese board highlights fresh flavors with marinated vegetables and creamy cheeses.

Ingredients:

- 4 oz of feta cheese (crumbled or block)
- 6 oz of manchego
- 4 oz of herbed goat cheese
- ½ cup of marinated olives
- ½ cup of roasted red peppers
- 1 cup of cucumber slices and cherry tomatoes
- Gluten-free flatbread crackers

Directions:

1. Arrange the feta, manchego, and herbed goat cheese in different areas of the board.
2. Add marinated olives and roasted red peppers around the cheeses.
3. Place cucumber slices and cherry tomatoes in clusters for freshness.
4. Include gluten-free flatbread crackers for pairing.

Beverage Pairings:
Pair with a dry rosé, sparkling water with lemon, or a Mediterranean white wine.

Fruit-Focused Nut-Free Cheese Board

This cheese board is rich in fresh and dried fruits to complement the variety of cheeses, making it both vibrant and allergy-friendly.

Ingredients:

- 4 oz of sharp white cheddar
- 6 oz of blue cheese
- 4 oz of gouda
- 1 cup of fresh figs and strawberries
- ½ cup of dried cranberries
- ½ cup of pumpkin seeds (nut-free alternative)
- Gluten-free crackers

Directions:

1. Place the cheeses on the board, spaced evenly apart.
2. Add fresh figs, strawberries, dried cranberries, and pumpkin seeds around the cheeses.
3. Fill in gaps with gluten-free crackers for pairing.

Beverage Pairings:
Pair with a sweet Riesling, sparkling berry-infused water, or a light Chardonnay.

Spicy Nut-Free Cheese Board

For spice lovers, this nut-free cheese board combines bold, fiery cheeses with fresh, crunchy accompaniments.

Ingredients:

- 4 oz of pepper jack cheese
- 6 oz of aged cheddar with chili flakes
- 4 oz of smoked gouda
- ½ cup of marinated jalapeños
- 1 cup of carrot and celery sticks
- ½ cup of roasted chickpeas (nut-free alternative)
- Gluten-free tortilla chips

Directions:

1. Arrange the pepper jack, cheddar, and smoked gouda on the board.
2. Add marinated jalapeños, carrot sticks, and celery sticks around the cheeses.
3. Include roasted chickpeas as a nut-free crunchy option.
4. Place tortilla chips on the edges for pairing.

Beverage Pairings:
Pair with a spicy margarita mocktail, a smoky mezcal cocktail, or sparkling water with lime.

Holiday Nut-Free Cheese Board

This festive nut-free cheese board features holiday-inspired flavors and colorful ingredients for a joyful centerpiece.

Ingredients:

- 4 oz of cranberry-studded white cheddar
- 6 oz of Parmesan wedges
- 4 oz of brie topped with fig jam
- 1 cup of fresh apple slices and pomegranate arils
- ½ cup of roasted sunflower seeds (nut-free alternative)
- Gluten-free seed crackers

Directions:

1. Place the brie in the center of the board and top it with fig jam.
2. Arrange the cranberry-studded cheddar and Parmesan wedges around the brie.
3. Add apple slices and pomegranate arils around the cheeses.
4. Include roasted sunflower seeds and seed crackers for pairing.

Beverage Pairings:
Pair with a sparkling white wine, a cranberry mocktail, or hot apple cider.

Printed in Dunstable, United Kingdom